4e

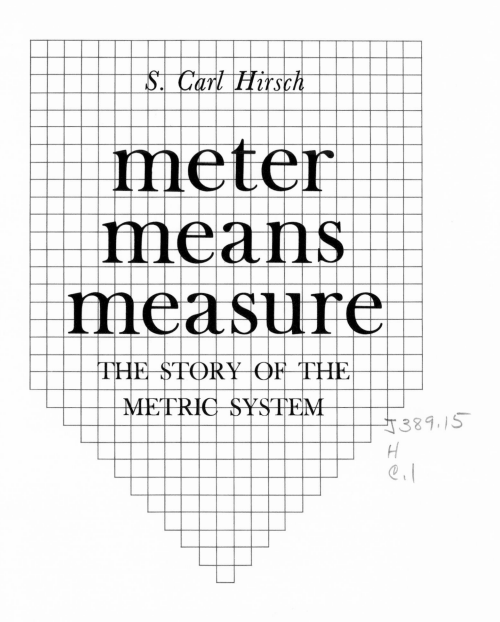

S. Carl Hirsch

meter
means
measure

THE STORY OF THE
METRIC SYSTEM

The Viking Press   *New York*

Copyright © 1973 by S. Carl Hirsch

All rights reserved
First published in 1973 by The Viking Press, Inc.
625 Madison Avenue, New York, N.Y. 10022
Published simultaneously in Canada by
The Macmillan Company of Canada Limited
Printed in U.S.A.

2   3   4   5   77   76   75   74

Library of Congress Cataloging in Publication Data

Hirsch, S. Carl
    Meter means measure.

    Bibliography: p.
    SUMMARY: Discusses the creation and development
of the metric system and explains why its adoption
by the United States is both inevitable and desirable.
    1. Metric system—Juvenile literature.
[1. Metric system. 2. Measuring]   I. Title.
QC92.5.H57   389'.152   72-91398
ISBN 0-670-47365-0

Also by S. Carl Hirsch

STILTS

THE RIDDLE OF RACISM

CITIES ARE PEOPLE

FOURSCORE . . . AND MORE:
THE LIFE SPAN OF MAN

GLOBE FOR THE SPACE AGE

GUARDIANS OF TOMORROW:
PIONEERS IN ECOLOGY

THE LIVING COMMUNITY:
A VENTURE INTO ECOLOGY

MAPMAKERS OF AMERICA

ON COURSE! NAVIGATING IN SEA, AIR, AND SPACE

PRINTING FROM A STONE:
THE STORY OF LITHOGRAPHY

THIS IS AUTOMATION

ACKNOWLEDGMENTS

First, thanks must go to the National Bureau of Standards at Gaithersburg, Maryland, where Louis E. Barbrow, Jeffrey V. Odom, and Roy E. Clark patiently briefed me in the Metric Study and later read the manuscript. I also appreciate the help of Daniel V. DeSimone, formerly director of the Metric Study Group.

Other helpful script readers were Marybelle Garrigan, Department of Curriculum, Chicago Board of Education; and Louis F. Sokol, President of the Metric Association, Inc. I appreciate assistance and encouragement from William S. Graybeal, Research Division, National Education Association; Maria Rae Glasgow, NEA Director for California; F. J. Helgren, metric educator; and Joseph R. Caravella, National Council of Teachers of Mathematics.

Useful assistance was supplied by G. D. Hughes, National Oceanic and Atmospheric Administration; P. C. Boire, Director, Metric Commission of Canada; Charles T. Mulcahy, Ford Motor Company; Donald L. Zylstra, National Aeronautics and Space Administration.

Finally, I would like to pay tribute to Velma V. Varner, Director and Editor of Junior Books, The Viking Press, who had read the manuscript of this book before her death in November 1972.

For Ruth Gregory
whose helpfulness turned written pages
into printed ones

CONTENTS

1 The Long and Short of It 9

2 The Measuring Mind 19

3 An American in Paris 25

4 Arc or Pendulum? 38

5 A Battle Begins 49

6 The Meter Finds a Home 60

7 Nature Sets a Standard 69

8 The Globe Turns Metric 80

9 A Unity of Units 94

10 Change Is Strange 106

———

Tables 118
Prefixes for Metric Units
Definitions of Basic Units
Common Conversion Factors
Suggestions for Further Reading 121
Index 122

THE LONG
AND SHORT
OF IT

A healthy American baby girl born in the year 2000 may tip the scales at exactly three kilograms—instead of 6.6 pounds. And her body temperature will undoubtedly read about 37 degrees—Celsius.

At school age, when she is perhaps 100 centimeters tall and drinks a liter of milk a day, she may ask her father, "Daddy, what was an inch?"

Inches and pounds will be remembered as something out of an earlier age. It will be recalled that such measurements were part of people's daily lives. It may seem odd in the new century that there were people in America who were once balky and fearful about changing to the metric system.

This country will know then that cars run as smoothly as ever on liters of gasoline; that there is nothing mysterious about kilograms on a bathroom scale; that in summer and winter the thermometer speaks just as plainly in Celsius degrees as it once did in Fahrenheit; that Americans can go anywhere in the world and be at home with the local language of measurement.

The change to the metric system does not turn everything topsy-turvy. American coinage, already decimal, remains the same. In their daily work machinists and mapmakers, grocers and weather forecasters may be greatly affected by the change; but for actors and social workers, florists and firemen, it is "business as usual."

The size of a football field need not be changed; railroads will go on running over tracks of the same gauge; a cake may still be put together by teaspoonsful and cupsful and pinches. Music will be played from the same notes arranged in the same measures. In the Blue Grass country the fine race horses will probably continue to run the eight furlongs and be measured as so many hands high.

However, the world has gone metric. And gradually metric measurement will become the everyday usage of Americans, as it already is for people around this globe.

The complete changeover in the United States will be troublesome and costly. But every other nation has found by experience that the advantages of the metric system far outweigh the expenses of the conversion, and the long-range improvements outrun any temporary confusion. Some of the benefits are

Trading a clumsy, patched-up, and out-of-date system of measurement for a simple, orderly one that is easier to teach and to learn in our schools.

Adopting measurements based on the decimal factor of ten that fits in neatly with our pattern of counting and our official coinage, both of which are also based on the decimal principle.

Improving chances for increased United States exports in a world market that produces and distributes, buys and sells in metric terms.

Familiarizing the general public with the language of measurement that has long been used universally by scientists.

Man's growing scientific knowledge of this earth is now being recorded not in miles but in meters, not in quarts but in liters, not in pounds but in kilograms.

In the early June days of 1972 delegates from one hundred and thirty countries met in Stockholm to take part in the United Nations Conference on the Human Environment. The nations decided to join in reckoning the sum of this earth's resources. They agreed to measure the dangers that threaten water, air, soil, and all living things, including man.

"Only One Earth" was the motto of the Stockholm conference, which focused the eyes of the world on the endangered environment. Thousands of scientists are now engaged in a thorough investigation of earth problems.

How do we apply to American cities the results of careful Japanese studies of air pollution in Tokyo and Osaka?

What useful information about saving Lake Erie can we gather from similar Russian studies on Lake Baikal and Kenyan research on Lake Nakaru? How can we best handle radio dispatches from the countries around the Caribbean, which sound early warnings about hurricanes approaching the North American coast? What can we learn from the giant water purification plants now operating in the Middle East?

Valuable new information is available to every nation trying to improve the quality of life for its people. All of this data is being compiled in metric units, terms which are used by scientists everywhere and understood by populations throughout the world, speaking in every tongue.

If the United States has been slow in learning and using this new language of measurement, this country is now catching up. The needs of our age are speeding America toward metric usage. The desire for more foreign trade, for international understanding, for solutions of the earth's environmental problems—these and other reasons point toward a metric America in a metric world. In the years just ahead all of humanity, including Americans, will be speaking one universal language of measurement.

The inch and the foot, the yard and the mile—such units no longer serve global needs. The meter has become the measure of the modern age.

Light on the Meter

What is a meter? Some may describe it as a unit of measure that is "a little longer than a yard." Others may say it is 39.37 inches.

However, the meter has been much more exactly defined

than that. Today's needs demand a unit of length that is fixed and accurate to the highest possible degree. The world has gone precise.

If a unit of length is to fulfill today's rigorous demands, there must be an unvarying model to which this unit can always be compared. But even the hardest metals known to man have proved to be unable to stand the test of time. No man-made object can retain its exact dimensions against the forces of weathering and wear, rust and rot, damage and destruction.

Only after a long search did scientists find a dependable standard with which to equate the meter. They discovered it in a gleam of light—in the special light that is given off by the atoms of an element called krypton-86. The length of one meter is equal to an established number of the wave lengths of this orange-red light.

Today the meter is the world's recognized unit of length. It is the fixed reference accepted not only by the so-called metric countries, but also by those few nations that have not yet changed completely to the metric system, including the United States. Legally, all United States units of length are related to the meter. According to law the yard is 0.9144 meters long.

The meter is the core of a scientifically planned system of measuring units. No system has ever been so complete. In no other system are the units of length, volume, weight, or mass linked together in such a harmonious design. Nor have any measuring units ever been more simple to use.

All measurement systems have a basic unit of length. In their search for a suitable unit of length, men of old adopted a bewildering array of different measuring units. In fact there were at one time almost as many varying units of length as there were sizes of men.

A Body of Measurements

Early man became a measuring man. As he began to build sound structures, make clothing, plant crops, engage in trade, reckon the distance of a journey, he needed a set of measuring units. Only then could he calculate in simple fashion and communicate his findings to his fellow man.

In its simplest form measuring is counting. Units are counted—whether they be yards or meters, pounds or kilograms. However, every measuring system must begin with a well-defined unit or a set of units. Each unit is a fixed quantity and is usually part of a scale of units, large and small. The scale of units of length in one measuring system includes inches, feet, yards, miles. In another system, the scale of units of length lists millimeters, centimeters, meters, kilometers.

Other scales in a measuring system are made up of units of volume, of weight or mass, of time, of temperature. The most important element of a measuring system is its basic unit of length.

A useful unit of length—what might it be? A single pace, perhaps? But a tall woman may take a longer step than a short man.

What about the girth of a man—could that be used as a fixed dimension? But whose waistline—that of a fat man or a lean man?

Or why not measure by the distance between a man's nose and the fingertips of his outstretched arm?

All of these have in fact been used at one time or another as units of length. They served in an age when men and women dealt only in crude measurements. Pacing was a way of measuring a field. A customer in a tavern ordered a drink of liquor by the number of digits, meaning the breadth of several fingers. And a housewife buying cloth might accept the nose-to-fingertip measure as a generous yard.

In order to become established, a system of measurement also needs standards. These are physical models of the units. A knotted cord or a notched stick might serve as a temporary standard of length for a small group of men building a bridge. However, a community or a nation needs units which are represented by commonly agreed and officially accepted standards.

In old-time measuring systems men often referred to parts of the human body as though they were of fixed dimensions. A human foot was actually considered the standard for the unit of length. Another commonly used measure, the fathom, also called the armstretch, was the distance between the fingertips of both hands when the arms are outstretched. A pinch was a quantity used not only by cooks but also by those who prepared medical remedies. The pinch was not very accurate, but it was handy.

The finger width and the handspan, the length of finger joints and of the forearm, which was also called a cubit— these were adopted as official standards for the units by which length was measured. The rod, it is said, was based on the total length of the shoeless right feet of the first sixteen men who came out of a church!

Using the human body as a measuring stick proved to be no simple solution. In any useful measuring system, there must be large and small units of length. But if the units were to be based on human dimensions, how could they be easily related to each other? There was no natural kinship between the size of a man's foot and the length of his arm.

Nevertheless, attempts were made to force them into a related scale of sizes. By stretching and squeezing, the smaller units were fitted evenly into the larger ones. But at best these were makeshift efforts to use human body measurements as a practical set of coherent units.

In one country, for example, five feet was considered to be equal to one double pace. And a mile (from the Latin word for one thousand) was a thousand double paces. One fathom became recognized as the equivalent of six feet. A man's girth (the old Anglo-Saxon word was *gyrd*) became a yard, or half a fathom. It was further decided that ten finger widths were the same as one span, the distance across two palms.

While such measures as these may have been adopted by one people, a neighboring people across a river or a ridge might well have chosen an entirely different set of units and standards.

In the past every civilization, society, and nation established its own ways of measuring. There are no longer any clear records which show the exact measures used in building the Great Wall of China, the Mayan temples, the Pyramids. But some old units of length such as the Egyptian cubit, the Anglo-Saxon yard, and the Roman mile were still being used in modern times.

Monarchs in various countries usually set standards of measurement. From the Pharaohs of Egypt to the kings of England, sovereigns laid down the rule of thumb by which men have measured, some using their own body dimensions as the fixed standards. When kings died or were overthrown, their tables of measurement often disappeared with them.

To add to the confusion, units varied with every language and in every land. Cities and towns had their own weights and measures. A traveler crossing Europe three hundred years ago reported that "the word 'pound' was applied to 391 differing units of weight and the word 'foot' to 282 unlike units of length."

A Time of Change

Outmoded measuring systems, like old habits, are hard to change. But as Europe emerged from the dim mists of the Middle Ages, the bright promise of new ideas was in the air.

The invention of printing would eventually bring education within the reach of the common man. World-wide trade and travel threw various peoples into closer touch with one another. As the seventeenth century began, a revolution in science was under way.

These and many other developments were altering old ways of life and thought. They would also give rise in time to a new system of measurement.

Pinning their faith on the writings of the past, most people of that era continued to believe in a motionless earth as the center around which celestial bodies floated through space. Wise men of old, they supposed, had reasoned out the fixed "divine plan" of the universe. On these ancient teachings people relied for everything they needed to know about the real world.

A few bold scientists had begun to question the old dogmas. They turned from the old writings to a new and direct examination of nature itself. Their method was to take nothing for granted. In order to learn the truth they observed patiently, and they recorded what they saw and measured in the world around them. New discoveries in science were based on experimentation to test each theory by precise measurement.

Gradually men began to feel the need for an orderly and exact and reasonable system of measuring units, linked by simple ratios, universally understood and accepted. The beginnings of that need can be traced back to events occurring almost four hundred years ago.

America was then a scattering of candlelit colonies and firelit Indian villages in a dark wilderness. In Europe, beyond the wide sea, the new light of learning had suddenly begun to glimmer and glow.

THE
MEASURING
MIND

During a religious service Galileo watched one of the huge lamps hanging on a long chain in the great Pisa cathedral. The glowing chandelier had somehow been set into motion and was swinging back and forth in a gradually increasing arc. The seventeen-year-old student suddenly became aware of the first of several remarkable facts about the motion of a pendulum.

Swaying to and fro, the chandelier kept pace perfectly with the measured beat of the music from the choir loft.

Even as the arc of the pendulum swings narrowed, its rhythm remained exactly the same.

When the music stopped, Galileo measured the rhythm of the swinging fixture against his own pulse beat. And still the interval of time required for one complete oscillation continued constant.

As he rushed homeward, the young student pondered a single question: was it true that the beat of a pendulum remains the same whether the pendulum swings through a wide arc or a narrow one?

In the days that followed, Galileo invented experiments to test and prove his hypothesis and to explore other questions about the behavior of pendulums. His studies made it clear that the pendulum is a useful device for measuring time and the force of gravity and led him to many other important discoveries about the motion of bodies.

In the closing years of the sixteenth century, modern science was being born. Those who gave it birth were bold experimenters who no longer blindly accepted unproved, traditional ideas about the natural world.

Essential to the new method was precise measurement. The main concern of the physical scientist, Galileo said, was the size, shape, quantity, and motion of objects—"those things capable of being measured." The new science would give rise eventually to a new system of measurement.

Because he challenged the dogmas of the past, Galileo ran the risk of being burned at the stake. But no threat could deter his quest for knowledge. The Italian scientist centered his attention on what he called "this immense book that nature keeps open before those who have eyes in their forehead and brains." The book was written, Galileo discovered, in the language of measurement.

Charting the Heavens

Early in the seventeenth century, Galileo corresponded with a German scientist on the motion of heavenly bodies. "It is deplorable," he wrote in Latin, "that there are so few who seek the truth." The letter was addressed to Johannes Kepler.

In his own country Kepler was regarded as a moody stargazer with strange ideas. He was persecuted by religious bigots. And he was hampered by old notions and superstitions concerning the universe. It was commonly believed that heavenly bodies moved by mysterious forces, unknown and forever unknowable.

Using painstaking observations and careful measurements, Kepler the astronomer helped to upset the false concept of a fixed earth at the center of the universe. Through the mind of this lonely and tormented man moved the great wheel of the heavens. He was not content to accept the old doctrines about the apparent movement of celestial objects.

Before he died Kepler offered mankind a master plan of the planets, the relationship of their paths and speeds, revealing the pattern of their motion around the sun.

Kepler wrote his own epitaph, which was later inscribed on his tombstone.

I was a measurer of the skies
Now I measure the earth's shadows.
In the skies was the measuring mind,
In the shadow lies only the body.

A Slight Error

Late into the nights a young Englishman sat in the garden of his family's country manor house, pondering Kepler's laws of planetary motion. He was Isaac Newton, sent home from college because of the plague which gripped all of England in the summer of 1665. He settled down for the next two years to wait out the deadly scourge, making the most of his time.

Young Newton was a quiet, brooding fellow, near-sighted and serious-minded. He spent little energy on sports or chores, both of which he disliked. Instead, he worked sleeplessly on his own scientific problems. He lived in a secret world of his own curiosities about the nature of the universe and the forces governing its motions.

Newton wondered whether the force of gravity that pulls objects to the earth extended as far as the moon. And now he was struck with a rather simple formula that might be used to measure the force of gravitation between two bodies—any two bodies in the universe.

The figures flew across the paper as young Newton applied his formula to the moon and the earth. But, alas, the results did not come out right. Despairing, the young scientist believed the discrepancy meant that his reasoning was faulty, and he threw the problem aside.

The source of the error, however, lay in an incorrect measurement of the earth itself. At that time a degree of latitude was thought to be equal to sixty English miles. And therefore Newton had used too small a figure in his formula for the radius of the earth. Still the problem gnawed at Newton's mind. A few years later he returned to it when a more accurate measurement had been made of the earth's circumference.

Before he was half finished calculating, Newton could see how the figures were running. Overcome with excitement, he called to a friend and asked him to complete the arithmetic. But Newton already knew that his formula for the force of gravitation had passed its first test!

Light Ends the Night

In the spreading light of the new era, both heaven and earth took on a startling clarity. The glow of bright and fresh ideas reaching out across Europe was later to be called the Enlightenment.

Life had its dark side as well. Senseless wars were being bitterly fought. Religious freedom was denied. Women were burned to death as witches. People still believed that the stars controlled their lives. Common folk slaved and starved in the grip of tyrants.

But just as age-old mysteries in nature were being solved, so the new ideas of the Enlightenment were also leading to social change—to a challenge of the divine right of kings. Everything left over from the past was being looked at anew from the viewpoint of human needs and human hopes.

With the expansion of trade the commerce between nations ran up against the barrier of differing units used locally in weighing and measuring goods.

It was a time of world exploration—and the seafarers of many nations sought to learn from each other the measuring arts of navigation.

In his laboratory the scientist viewed the world with new

and keen insights. The scientific style of work now included careful measurement, carried on with increasingly improved instruments.

Space and time, mass and force—these could be reduced to numbers, quantities. The large heavenly bodies and the small particles of matter could be measured and their motions predicted. All of nature was seen as understandable and measurable. Order in the universe was no longer viewed as a matter of simple faith but of scientific formulas which might be tested and verified.

Suddenly science was international. The discoveries in one nation were made available to fellow scientists everywhere. Across great distances students checked the works of others and added their own findings. The era was bursting with new scientific investigations—in the manner of Galileo, Kepler, and Newton. Direct measurement was a vital part of their method of confirming or refuting theories.

Research in the eighteenth century was hindered not only by the shortcomings of the measuring tools but also by the lack of a clear and uniform measuring system. Learned men from various lands wrote in Latin so that they might better understand each other. And in time they would also seek a common language of measurement. But meanwhile the flow of scientific information was hampered by the need to translate and convert data from one system of measurement into another.

The confusion over differing systems of measurements troubled not only scientists and scholars, but also ordinary people in everyday life. In France and England and in the newborn United States, merchants and mechanics, farmers and statesmen worried over what was called weights and measures. The problem weighed heavily on the mind of Thomas Jefferson.

AN AMERICAN
IN PARIS

The summer night had turned sultry. Thomas Jefferson tested the wind with a moistened forefinger. He wagered the ship's captain that there was not enough stir in the air to carry the *Ceres* out of Boston Harbor and onto the high seas. It was July 4, 1784. Jefferson was bound for France as United States minister. The American Revolution was only a few years behind him. The French Revolution would break out in full fury just a few years ahead.

In the lantern light, beaver skins in bundles of ten were being passed hand to hand by the men loading the ship.

"Eight tens. Nine tens. A hundred." The captain counted aloud as the last of the cargo moved steadily toward the hold.

For days, weeks, Jefferson had been absorbed with the way men count and reckon. In some primitive time early man had invented a system of numbers. His ever-ready computer was his own ten fingers or toes. This was the simplest reckoning method—counting fingers, then repeating the process. Jefferson recalled that this was the same method he had learned as a child in a Virginia school. "Count to ten, then start over again."

In ancient times many tribes used the fingers of only one hand, counting by fives. A few counted by twenties, apparently using the digits of both hands and both feet as well. But somehow the system based on ten numbers survived the longest. The decimal system, with a number base of ten, was the most common of all counting schemes.

It was this thought that turned uppermost in Jefferson's mind when the government of the United States called on him to devise a system of coinage and of weights and measures for the newborn nation.

The moneys being used then in America were a jangling tangle of confusion. Most people couldn't make head or tail out of it all. Spanish and English, French and Portuguese coins passed from hand to hand, and few Americans had any notion of their fixed worth. In addition the individual colonies had minted their own currencies in a perplexing range of sizes, shapes, and values.

The weights and measures were in even more of a muddle. The confusion caused endless problems for the new nation. Trade and commerce were hindered. People became easy prey for cheats and swindlers.

A crafty merchant might use one kind of pound weight on his scale for buying butter from a farmer and a different pound weight in selling the same butter to a housewife. A bushel of oats was not measured out of the same size bushel in Kentucky as it was in Virginia or Connecticut. Even the United States custom-houses at various ports along the coast used different weights on their scales, so that shippers preferred to dock at whichever port charged them the lowest duty.

A confusing array of containers had become the units of capacity. Goods were sold by the box, the barrel, the bottle, the bale, the bag, the basket, the bucket, the bushel. But as to the actual quantity of contents—let the buyer beware!

Jefferson was wisely chosen to lead the United States out of the mess. The Virginian was a man who loved order and had a talent for finding it.

Within a few months, in between a hundred other major duties, Jefferson put together a new plan for United States coinage. He finished it while he was packing to sail for Europe. Jefferson's money system was to become a model for all the world, as easily understood as it was useful.

The dollar was to be the new standard of United States money. There would be a simple decimal ratio between the dollar and all other pieces of money in both larger and smaller denominations. In adopting Jefferson's system of "dollars, dimes and cents," the nation agreed with his reasoning.

To begin with, the commonly used counting system was based on the number ten. Then why not tie all other systems to the same decimal factor, with its clear and simple ratios? The arithmetic of tens was used throughout the world, and no other system lent itself to such easy reckoning.

Take, for example, that remarkable little device—the decimal point. One could multiply or divide by ten, a hundred, or a thousand simply by moving the decimal point the appropriate number of places in the proper direction. As for adding and subtracting, the decimal system was by far the speediest and least troublesome.

Jefferson wanted a system so easy to use that not even a child would be likely to err or be cheated. "The bulk of mankind," he pointed out, "are school boys thro' life."

Having completed his proposal for a coinage system, the Virginian embarked for Europe with a light heart. It was his idea that with decimals well established in his country's coinage, it later would be easy to introduce the same factor of ten "into the kindred branches of weights and measures."

Strangely, his best efforts were to end with zero.

Jacks and Jills

It was daybreak when Jefferson's ship at last got underway, and he watched the last lights of the Boston shore dim and die out. Through the next summery days of the Atlantic crossing he was a man suddenly set free from the cares of statesmanship.

The ship's captain found the Virginian to be the most fascinating of his six passengers. Jefferson studied the sea and the sky, followed the flight of petrels and shearwaters, fished for cod on a becalmed day, and taught himself Spanish between times.

A friend once described Jefferson as an amazing person who "could calculate an eclipse, survey an estate, tie an artery, plan an edifice, try a case, break a horse, dance a minuet, and play a violin."

An amateur scientist with an inquiring mind, Jefferson had taught himself to observe and reason in the scientific manner. He was a zealous student of the enlightened ideas of his age. And since science was now absorbed with exact measurement, it is clear why Jefferson was so concerned about the sorry state of the weights and measures in his own country.

America's jumble of measuring units and standards was mainly a hand-me-down from the mother country, England. Americans copied Englishmen in matters of speech, dress, and customs. They also walked an English league, sold their corn by the Winchester bushel, bought snuff by the pennyweight, and drank their ale by the English pint.

As a schoolboy, Jefferson was given a list of English units to memorize that boggled his mind. In a typical classroom scene of those days the schoolmaster would take a deep breath and then sing out the following ditty:

Two mouthfuls are a jigger; two jiggers are a jack; two jacks are a jill; two jills are a cup; two cups are a pint; two pints are a quart; two quarts are a pottle; two pottles are a gallon; two gallons are a pail; two pails are a peck; two pecks are a bushel; two bushels are a strike; two strikes are a coomb; two coombs are a cask; two casks are a barrel; two barrels are a hogshead; two hogsheads are a pipe; two pipes are a tun—and there my story is done!

Yet this was only a part of the staggering table of units, which also included fluid ounces and fluid drams, pennyweights and minims, grains and scruples. There were in use at least three systems of what were called weights—avoirdupois for bulky goods, troy for precious metals, and apothecaries' for tiny amounts. By custom, these were simply differing units used for weighing out quantities of flour, of gold, of medicine.

If anything, the units of length and area were even more mystifying. Moreover, there was hardly a trade or craft that did not have its own system. The printer measured in picas, the jeweler in carats, the horseman in furlongs, the woodcutter in cords, the surveyor in chains, the seaman in knots.

Any student who was not yet stupefied by this hodgepodge might ponder the hundredweight, which was usually 112 pounds but might be anything from 100 to 120 pounds. And there was not only the ton, but the long ton as well. And also the ounce, which might be either twelve or sixteen to the pound if the substance being measured was dry, or either sixteen or twenty to the pint for fluids.

Little wonder that Jefferson dreamed of a plain and common system of measurement, based on simple decimal ratios!

Frankly eager for help, the Virginian looked to Europe as the source of those "improvements in science, in arts and in civilization" which he had long admired from a distance. He knew that England was not satisfied with its traditional weights and measures. France was actively working on an entirely new system. What could be learned from these two countries to which the United States was so closely linked?

The *Ceres,* a new and fast ship, had made a remarkably swift crossing. In the early morning of the nineteenth day

Jefferson came up from his cabin to catch the fresh scent of salt air, the pungent smell of the ship's new cordage and canvas. As he had every morning of the voyage, the Virginian checked the ship's position and its course, the temperature and the wind direction. Land was now in sight and the light of a new day appeared on the eastern horizon.

France in Flux

In Paris Jefferson found delight in the store windows, craftsmen's shops, music halls, and scientific laboratories.

To his friends back home he sent pocket telescopes, a novel type of lamp, watches, a variety of finely made measuring instruments, and the new phosphorous-tipped matches, which offered "the convenience of lighting a candle without getting out of bed."

For himself Jefferson purchased a small instrument, which he strapped to his leg. The pedometer ticked off the paces to the French mile and Jefferson was able to calculate that his stride was exactly 30.6 English inches long.

As Jefferson wandered about the old city, the signs of grinding poverty were everywhere. A corrupt nobility had ruled France for centuries. They lived extravagantly while high taxes were wrung from the common folk.

Embittered Frenchmen brooded over a long list of grievances. Among them was the abuse of a confusing and unreliable system of weights and measures. The people felt they were being cheated in everything they bought or sold.

Familiar with the popular mood of rebellion, Jefferson could see where France was heading. His own country had been fired with the same spirit. The ideas of the Enlightenment had kindled the need for democratic change. Paris seethed with intimations of popular revolution.

Jefferson, convinced that their cause was just, mixed freely among the people throughout the tumult and strife. The American felt safe and at home among Frenchmen.

Jefferson's Declaration of Independence was not only enshrined in American hearts, but was also well known to every European revolutionist. Writing home about France, Jefferson declared, "Its inhabitants love us more, I think, than they do any other nation on earth."

On a bright, midsummer morning, Jefferson went to the Arsenal of Paris to visit the great French chemist Antoine Lavoisier. The two men had much in common. They were born in the same year. In fact, they were typical sons of the new scientific age. Moreover, they were drawn together by a common interest in weights and measures.

Lavoisier had his home and his splendid laboratory in the Arsenal. As a member of the Royal Academy of Sciences, the chemist was obliged to do a good deal of the government's scientific work. He did research and testing, and prepared reports on a wide variety of matters—new lamps, inks, gunpowder, soaps, coinage, manufacturing processes, foods, and inventions, including a new device designed by Dr. Joseph Ignace Guillotin, a "painless" way to put criminals to death.

Lavoisier had helped to transform the science of chemistry on entirely new and modern foundations. Jefferson, who was especially interested in this science, was also excited about Lavoisier's views on a new plan of measurement. As a leading advocate of a universal system, the chemist envisioned that "it would be understood in all countries as well as in all languages."

To Lavoisier, the main problem was the selection of a suitable unit of length. Such a unit, once chosen, would then become the basis for defining other units—area, volume, mass. All the scales of units would be linked by the decimal factor of ten.

Another problem had to do with finding proper standards —accurate models of each of the basic units in some permanent, physical form.

Lavoisier was then director of the committee to establish the new system of measurements. He told Jefferson that he was testing copper, platinum, and various other metals in order to determine which was best suited for use in making durable standards of length and mass. Through the passage of time, changes in temperature, chemical interaction, handling and wear took their toll on even the hardest substances known to man. What kind of metal bar could forever represent for the world a fixed, unvarying standard for the unit of length?

Lavoisier devoted much time to the gram, which he proposed as the fundamental unit of mass in the new system. The unit would be based on a certain quantity of water, the precise amount needed to fill a cube with each side equal to the fundamental unit of length. But what kind of water? Sea water, rain water, distilled water, or water out of the River Seine? Each showed a different mass on Lavoisier's delicate and precision balances. Even the same kind of water at different temperatures did not weigh the same.

In the laboratory of the brilliant French chemist Jefferson came to understand the kind of scientific effort needed to devise a new system of measurement. Lavoisier's laboratory was one of the finest and best equipped in the world.

A watchword of this time of upheaval called for freedom

in pursuing the search for knowledge. The Enlightenment had encouraged men to take nothing for granted, to question, examine, challenge every old idea.

Lavoisier and Jefferson were closely matched in their scientific views. If the two men had any major difference, it was in their political views. Jefferson was fully committed to democratic government. Lavoisier favored moderate reforms, but he believed that the French monarchy could be saved.

Besides being a great chemist, Lavoisier was skillful in financial matters. He had built himself a large personal fortune as a partner in an enterprise called the Farmers General. Licensed by the crown to collect all taxes, Lavoisier's company was bitterly hated by the French people. In the stormy period ahead the aroused populace was to weigh in the scales of justice Lavoisier, the scientist who revolutionized chemistry, and Lavoisier, the king's tax collector.

As for Jefferson, diplomatic matters soon took him to England. That country too had its "weights and measures" in the balance.

Mother Country

To England Jefferson traced more than just his own family roots. Here too was the soil in which many American customs had grown.

Most Americans still retained English manners and habits even after the bitterly fought War of Independence. Perhaps because they won, the Yankees were quick to forgive. But having lost, the English nursed their ill will.

Jefferson presented himself to King George III, only to have the monarch turn his back on the American patriot.

Wherever he went during his seven weeks in Great Britain, he found a lack of "common good manners" toward him.

His diplomatic mission was a failure. Still Jefferson was able to use the opportunity to check on some of the scientific matters that were of great interest to him.

In this land of the great Isaac Newton, measurement had indeed become very precise. Jefferson purchased a large number of fine British-made instruments. He visited the great observatory at Greenwich, which had pioneered in establishing a universal system of measuring longitude. He also met with scholars who were "fellow worshippers in the temple of science."

Among them was James Watt, the man whose remarkable steam engine was powering mines, mills, and factories in the English Industrial Revolution. Since his early days as a maker of scientific measuring instruments, the Scottish Watt had been a gruff and outspoken critic of the cumbersome English system of weights and measures. He urged that nations scrap the entire accumulation of ancient measuring units and begin afresh.

However, as a people wedded firmly to their traditions, the British seemed little interested in what other countries were doing to bring about a new world-wide system of measurements.

England, Jefferson noted, was still using the pound as both a unit of weight and a unit of money. That practice had its origin several thousand years before in the wealthy Mediterranean kingdom of Lydia. There the first gold and silver coins were minted and stamped with their weight. These coins were not only circulated as a medium of exchange, but were also used as standards of weight in the scales and balances of the ancient world.

From the Mediterranean this practice traveled northward with the invading Roman legions almost 2000 years ago. In England it appeared as the pound. The Latin word for pound, *libra,* was abbreviated as "lb.," and this symbol became widely used in English-speaking countries.

The foot and the mile as units of length also marched into Britain in ancient times. The conquering Romans imposed their measuring standards upon England under Julius Caesar's rule. When the English later built their own world-wide empire, they too introduced the foot wherever their flag appeared. That was how America came to be measured in feet.

The Romans marked off the mile not in terms of feet but as 1000 double paces. Over the years, the mile as defined in various countries was stretched and strained to the point where no one really knew where it might end. That, unfortunately, was the story of all units of measurement which were not pegged to a precise and permanent standard. In time the English mile came to have as many as 5280 feet. British sea captains used the nautical mile of 6080 feet.

Traveling in Europe, Jefferson was struck anew by the need for a universal agreement on weights and measures. As he crossed each national border, he found himself in a new realm of measurement. Pounds, feet, miles were generally used as units—but in each country they represented different values.

The mile was especially confusing. Jefferson found that country by country the national mile might be as short as 3600 feet or as long as 36,000 feet. In his travels Jefferson encountered the Tuscan mile, which was quite different from the Italian mile. The Swiss mile was longer than either. He found that some of his traveling companions along the Rhine used the German short mile while others figured distance in the German long mile.

If the number of feet in a mile varied, so also did the number of inches in a foot. The inch itself was of many sizes. Jefferson discovered that to some people it was a middle-finger width; to others the length of the first joint of the thumb. An English edict laid down at some long-forgotten time defined the inch as the length of "three barleycorns, round and dry."

The foot represented an amazing range of human feet, big and small. The Roman foot was twelve inches. In fact, the words "inches" and "ounces" had their origin in a Latin term meaning "one-twelfth." However, people in various European countries measured nine, ten, twelve, and sixteen inches to the foot. Both in England and America, the foot remained approximately the same—twelve inches— because of custom more than by law.

Perhaps his trip abroad convinced Jefferson that changing the system of measurement in England or in his own country would be no simple matter. Other countries might adopt new units of length. But the English-speaking world stood firmly on feet!

ARC
OR
PENDULUM?

At high noon Thomas Jefferson stared at the tall clock in New York's City Tavern. It was not the clock face but the swinging pendulum that held his attention.

In that cold wet spring of 1790 Jefferson was his country's new Secretary of State. At some later time the State Department became specialized in the nation's foreign affairs. But in those days it handled a variety of responsibilities. And Jefferson's main duty at the moment was to propose a new plan of "weights and measures."

New York City was then the temporary capital of the United States. And Jefferson's lodgings were a tiny room in a public tavern on Broadway. This was an uncomfortable place to work at the detailed report which he was preparing for Congress. The books and papers he needed for his research were either left behind in Paris or at his home in Virginia.

To make matters worse, his head throbbed with pain. For weeks a pounding headache came on every morning and stayed with him until sunset. Feet and yards, pints and gallons danced wildly across his mind while he tried to figure out some clear, sensible way to deal with an unbelievably complex problem. At night, when his brain cleared somewhat, he worked late by candlelight, trying to pull his thoughts together.

The Secretary of State tried to focus his attention on the unit at length. To Americans the foot with which they measured was as familiar as the feet on which they walked. But to Jefferson's way of thinking the foot could only become a reliable unit of measurement if there were some way of defining its length in terms of an unchanging standard found in nature.

In talks with his friends the Virginian discussed a plan based on his research. He suggested that a pendulum with a particular beat might be used as the model for a precise and steadfast unit of length. It was Galileo who had discovered that the time it takes a pendulum to complete its full swing is governed by the length of the pendulum.

Jefferson went back to Isaac Newton's writings for further facts. The great English physicist had determined that the bob of a pendulum completes its full swing in one second of time if it is hung on a string about 39 inches long.

Why not redefine the foot in terms of the length of a pendulum beating seconds?

Instead of a pendulum with a bob Jefferson favored the idea of using a slender iron rod, suspended at one end to allow it to swing freely. In order to tick off seconds such a rod, he calculated, would have to be 58.72368 inches long. Jefferson proposed to arrive at the new foot by dividing that long rod into five equal parts. He believed he now had discovered a workable unit of length, based on a dependable standard.

Some problems still needed to be solved. Since the beat of a pendulum of fixed length varies slightly from place to place, depending on the force of gravity, a specific location had to be chosen in setting up the pendulum standard. Furthermore, the pendulum rod, like all pieces of metal, would be affected by temperature changes.

The French were at that moment running into their own problems in their search for a standard of length "taken from nature."

Earth's Girth

In a later age men would venture to the bottom of the sea and into outer space. But the bold scientific undertaking of the 1790s was the exact measurement of the earth.

On the soggy beaches of France's northern coast two surveyors worked against overpowering difficulties. It was not only that fog blinded their instruments and storms hindered their movements, but that France was in the midst of a revolution.

The countryside was in turmoil. War threatened from

abroad as well, and the people were in fear of an invasion across the English Channel.

The two luckless surveyors, peering through telescopes, were taken for either royalist or foreign spies. Many times they found themselves in jail, waiting for word from Paris that they were indeed innocent men doing important government work. Repeatedly they were surrounded by mobs of wary peasants who threatened them with pitchforks.

They aroused suspicion by using signal flags which were white, the official color of the royal court. In fact, the unit in which they measured was called *pied-de-roi,* literally, "the foot of the king."

With the government changing almost daily, the survey party had trouble getting its pay. From time to time, the men had comforting letters from their superior in Paris, Antoine Lavoisier. But soon they learned that he, too, was under suspicion.

Nevertheless, the survey went on. Lavoisier eagerly pressed forward the earth-measuring project. What his committee hoped to achieve was a highly accurate reckoning of the arc between the Equator and the North Pole on the meridian passing through Paris. That arc, representing one quarter of the earth's circumference, would be divided by ten million to establish the new unit of length—the meter.

The plan of the surveyors was to verify the entire length of the meridian by the exact measurement of a given portion of it. Their overland survey took them from Dunkirk, France, to Barcelona, Spain, both of them sea-level cities on the Paris meridian.

Perhaps the choice of France as the site for the survey was not a wise one. Hatreds and fears in Europe were running strong at this time. Acceptance of the new measurement ideas would be hampered for many years by jealousy and suspicion among rival nations.

Even Jefferson shook his head sadly at hearing the reports from France. The French seemed to be saying to the world that the standard of measurement could be "found in no other country on earth but theirs," Jefferson remarked. The Secretary of State was also hearing the loud voices of America's English-minded merchants, and he realized what an outcry they would make against any proposal identified as French.

At that time in England a serious debate was going on in Parliament over changing the official weights and measures. The British were also pondering a new and "natural" unit of measurement. They considered the length of a pendulum that beats seconds of time and also the distance equivalent to one degree of latitude. Another proposal for a new unit of length was the interval spanned by a falling body in one second of time. As the unit of mass, British scientists suggested the amount of matter in a single drop of water.

The French were now appealing vigorously to all nations to join them in an effort to find a suitable common plan. But many American and English statesmen shunned the notion of a partnership with the unstable French government of the moment. The news from France was full of political turmoil.

There the cry for liberty was being drowned out at times by the call for revenge. In republican France the people had turned on the hated tyrants and profiteers, the jailers and tax collectors. Lavoisier, a leading designer of the new metric system, was among those arrested, Jefferson learned. The guillotine was soon to end his life.

A courier, Citizen Dombey, was dispatched from France

to invite America to a meeting of nations on measurement. He was shipwrecked during a hurricane in the Caribbean, captured and held prisoner by pirates. Citizen Dombey's papers were lost. He died without ever reaching the United States. The international meeting he was supposed to arrange never took place.

Meanwhile, Jefferson had completed his own plan.

Matter of Choice

July 4 was a date that was to ring a bell throughout Jefferson's life. On July 4, 1790, he turned over to the Congress of the United States his masterly report on "weights and measures."

It was two plans, not one. This designer of American democracy was not only outspoken in favor of free choices for the people, he believed in them as well. And while he disliked the disorder in America's old system of measuring, he was not sure the nation was ready for a completely new one. His report left that decision to the people and their government.

Jefferson hung his hopes on a long iron rod—the pendulum of exactly the correct length to beat in precise seconds of time. In his report he tried to deal with all its shortcomings as a fixed standard. Let it beat at 45 degrees latitude, he said, and at sea level. Keep it in a cellar, he added, or some other place where the temperature "never varies."

The foot, based on such a pendulum, would not be a perfect unit of length, Jefferson admitted. But it would be far more uniform than those which had existed in the past. He believed also that there was less uncertainty about the pendulum rod than about the actual length of the earth's meridian as the basis for the standard of length.

Jefferson suggested to Americans that in their measurements they "reduce every branch to the same decimal ratio already established in their coins." He hoped that this would bring "the calculation of the principal affairs of life within the arithmetic of every man who can multiply or divide plain numbers."

The Virginian's master plan then unfolded a set of linear measurements, all related to each other by "the rule of tens":

> 10 points make 1 line
> 10 lines make 1 inch
> 10 inches make 1 foot
> 10 feet make 1 decad
> 10 decads make 1 rood
> 10 roods make 1 furlong
> 10 furlongs make 1 mile

The units for area and volume would simply be squares and cubes of the units for length. The plan stressed "harmony" between the measurements. The factor of ten would apply not only to units of length but also to the units of weight or mass. Jefferson offered a basic ounce equivalent to a cubic inch of rain water. He suggested also that the size and weight of United States coins be related to the units of measurement as part of the same system.

Thus, in Plan No. 1, the Secretary of State proposed a complete revolution in weights and measures. In Plan No. 2 he suggested a series of mild reforms, the idea being to make the old system simpler and clearer.

Jefferson was willing to accept the partial plan. But he was hoping that the people were ready for a total change. He reasoned that "if our fellow citizens were ripe for advancing so great a length toward reformation, they would probably be ripe for taking the whole step." But he added, "Perhaps I was wrong."

Congressmen hailed the report as an excellent piece of work, even brilliant. That they did nothing about it is one of the mysteries of the time.

The seventy-year-old President, George Washington, urged them to act on this important matter. Congress still dawdled. Even when Jefferson became president, he was unable to move the congressmen into action. The legislators failed to make a choice between Jefferson's two plans. Rather, they chose not to choose.

In that time of unsettled world relationships there seemed to be little chance of bringing about any cooperation among the nations in securing a universal measuring system. The congressmen were also well aware that any tampering with weights and measures would bring an uproar from some of the solid citizens back home. Any change and the congressmen would be likely to hear from the whale-oil merchant filling hogsheads, the cotton grower packing bales, the farmer trading by the bushel, the mechanic marking off the English inch, the realtor still selling land measured in feet according to an old system called "metes and bounds."

Jefferson's report gathered dust. Periodically, he made the trip from his home, Monticello, to see if he could stir Congress into action. He kept track of his mileage by a new invention, an odometer, which he had attached to his carriage. This instrument rang a bell every mile and also recorded the mileage in tenths and hundredths. Whenever he was asked about his odometer, Jefferson was able to check on how well people responded to a decimal system of measurement.

The Virginian wrote to a friend: "The people on the road inquire with curiosity what exact distance I have found from such a place to such a place. I answer, so many miles, so many cents. I find they universally and at once form a perfect idea of the relation of the cent to the mile as a unit. They would do the same as to yards of cloth, pounds of shot, ounces of silver, or of medicine."

Instead of becoming a model for the entire world Jefferson's report aged and died in a forgotten pigeonhole. As one of the great statesman's biographers later wrote: "Thus Jefferson lost a title to fame which he might have cherished more than any of the political honors he gained or the offices he held."

In his report Jefferson had looked forward wistfully "to a future time when the citizens of the United States may be induced to undertake a thorough reformation of their whole system of measures, weights and coins."

Jefferson probably did not realize how far into the future he was looking.

Enter the Meter

A stormy century was coming to a close. On December 10, 1799, the meter was officially unveiled to the world.

On this occasion there were many lofty speeches in the gilded palaces of Paris where Napoleon now ruled. And there were many learned reports on how the meridian of the globe had been measured in order to determine the meter's length.

But the committee of French, Dutch, Italian, and Swiss scientists did not stop at defining the meter as a fixed portion of the earth's circumference. They also had the practical good sense to present the world with an iron bar representing the length of the meter.

In time finer meter bars were forged out of harder materials. But the metal bar remained for years the model of the meter.

However, the meter itself was simply the chief building block of a complete system of measurement that was now revealed in its grand design. Based on the factor of ten, the system was arranged in clear, orderly steps, all related to the meter. The system was an interlocking, coherent whole. As steps between larger and smaller units, the decimal factor was used throughout.

In fact, revolutionary France had been quite carried away with the decimal idea. They had tried to apply it also to the clock, the compass, and the calendar. Little of this survived—and for a very simple reason. The world was already in accord on a method of telling time, of reckoning directions, and of dividing the year. Being almost universal, these types of measurements did not need revision.

Nevertheless, for a brief period, the French struggled with the so-called republican calendar, in which the new year began with September 22, the autumnal equinox and also the first day after the founding of the French Republic in 1792. Every tenth day was a day of rest. Colorful and descriptive new names were given to the months, such as *Floréal* (flowery) for April–May, *Thermidor* (hot) for

July–August, *Brumaire* (foggy) for October–November, and *Nivôse* (snowy) for December–January.

An effort was made to reckon time in decimal divisions. The week was split into exactly a million parts. Ten days in a week, ten hours in a day, one hundred minutes in an hour, one hundred seconds in a minute—that was how the Republic proposed to tell time.

It took ten years for revolutionary France to learn that it was not necessary to overthrow everything that was old. Neither Frenchmen nor any other people could be convinced of the need for a new timetable.

Change, even for the better, comes hard and slow. And the metric system was not eagerly adopted by other nations of the world. The metric committee, centered in Paris, made vigorous and repeated appeals to all nations. Mankind, they believed, had now made a significant advance in the long search for better methods of acquiring knowledge. They also viewed the metric system as "capable of becoming a new link of universal brotherhood among all peoples who adopt it."

However, conditions had become dark and threatening once again. France and England were preparing for armed conflict. The Napoleonic wars were about to sweep across Europe. The United States was in dispute with France over its possessions in North America and was also moving toward war with England. In the turmoil the metric system was all but forgotten.

In September 1805 an immigrant arrived in Philadelphia with the idea of founding a Swiss colony in South Carolina. In his baggage he carried an iron bar. That was how the meter first came to America.

A BATTLE
BEGINS

Disaster greeted the Swiss immigrant Ferdinand Rudolph Hassler the moment he set foot in America. The land dealers from whom he had purchased the site for a farming colony turned out to be swindlers.

Hassler had to tell his one hundred and twenty fellow Swiss colonists that they were now stranded in a strange country, penniless and landless. Hassler himself and his family survived by selling off his books and scientific instruments. In order to buy food he even sold his precious iron bar, a duplicate standard of the meter, as well as a metal standard of the kilogram, another basic unit of the metric system.

Perhaps Hassler's dream of a rural colony would have come to nothing. Years later he would finally learn by his mistakes that he was unsuited to a farmer's life. Hassler had, in fact, much more to offer America as a scientist.

Geometry, geology, geography, geodesy—the *geo* portion of these terms is the Greek word for "earth." And in the early nineteenth century, these earth sciences flourished. Measurement and mapping of the planet, or portions of it, were the specialties of Ferdinand Hassler.

It was Thomas Jefferson, ever on the lookout for scientific talent, who hired Hassler. The Swiss scientist was put in charge of what was later called the United States Coast and Geodetic Survey. By law he was assigned to make "an accurate chart" of the entire shoreline of the United States.

When the Congressmen said "accurate" in 1807, Hassler took them at their word. In this fledgling nation, however, there were no instruments good enough for making a precise measurement of the Atlantic coast. Hassler took off for Europe in search of the proper equipment.

A year, two years, eight years passed before Hassler was ready to set up his first survey marker on the Long Island beach. He had long since run out of time and money. Congress had run out of patience.

The legislators demanded maps, large numbers of them. But they had no idea with whom they were dealing. Hassler was an unusual man, gifted, proud and hot-tempered. First and foremost he was a scientist devoted to precise measurement. His style of work was painstaking and methodical—

and let no one rush him or interfere with him! He could be prickly as a hedgehog.

Hassler was to be seen occasionally on the streets of Washington, D.C., in his homemade carriage. Drawn by four horses, this clumsy vehicle was Hassler's survey station and sleeping quarters in the field. It was built to provide easy riding for the scientist's delicate instruments. A built-in "cellar" held his books and records, as well as a tinkling music box to keep him company as he worked late into the night. Under the seats of the carriage were cabinets for Hassler's good Swiss wine, crackers, and cheese.

The members of Congress roared with laughter at the reports of Hassler's odd behavior—when they weren't furious about his finicky habits. As for the scientist, he was in a constant rage about the failure of Congress to adopt the metric system.

Hassler was certain that world-wide metric usage was only a matter of time. In Europe he had learned how helpful the new method was in his own work. The high-spirited Mr. Hassler was not going to let a "do-nothing" Congress stand in his way.

With a grand flourish of his pen Hassler signed an order that made the meter the fundamental unit for the entire coastal survey. All the maps of his bureau would be based on the metric system. Singlehandedly, Ferdinand Rudolph Hassler nudged the United States down the metric path.

During his long and turbulent career Hassler was fired and rehired. He nettled the nerves of five presidents and tangled fiercely with Congress through many skirmishes. But no one ever dared to challenge his integrity as a scientist. In his offices could be found the largest concentration of scientific talent in America. All of the nation's muddled problems with weights and measures were unloaded on his little agency, the United States Coast and Geodetic Survey. And Hassler's bureau became a hotbed of activity in behalf of the metric system.

But no one man or small group of men could turn the United States into a metric nation. Nor was the story any different in the European countries.

The People Decide

A towering statue overlooked the bustling Dalmatian seaport of Dubrovnik. The figure was that of Roland, a romantic hero of a bygone day.

For centuries the statue had provided the people with a simple standard of measurement. In that land the recognized unit of length was the distance from the bronze elbow of Roland to the first knuckles of his hand.

But in the year 1809 the thunder of guns signaled a change. Napoleon's armies were overrunning Europe. And the Little Corporal who had become an emperor laid down new rules in the lands he conquered.

Like many of the old laws, old units of measurement were declared illegal. In Dalmatia the merchants and carpenters, the farmers and fishermen were forbidden to measure according to Roland's arm.

Wherever Napoleon's tricolored flags fluttered, there the metric system became official.

It is one thing for a conqueror to give orders and quite another for the people to obey. A government may perhaps force people to use the coinage which it issues and controls, but the people will find some way of using measurements that meet their needs.

Napoleon's effort to impose the metric system on the people of Europe by force was short-lived. In many countries metric measurement came and went as quickly as did Napoleon's invading armies.

Even in France the new way of measuring was slow to take hold. Once again, Napoleon issued a decree. This time he ordered that the use of the meter would not be strictly enforced, that people could use a measuring system that was part old and part new.

Napoleon's order threw France into utter confusion. Getting used to a new system was hard enough. Using two systems was hopeless.

With such disorder the metric plan barely survived. As a defender of metric measurement, Napoleon undoubtedly did the cause more harm than good.

In spite of Napoleon, however, a few European countries voluntarily adopted the metric system. France's neighbors, Belgium, the Netherlands, Luxembourg, parts of Switzerland, and Italy were the first to go metric. And there matters paused during the first decades of the nineteenth century.

In the United States a few restless Congressmen worried over a measurement muddle that could only grow worse with time. This nation had reached a fork in the road, the legislators believed. What system of measurement for America—new French or old English? The Congressmen asked the opinion of the Secretary of State, John Quincy Adams.

"The meter will surround the globe," predicted Adams, "and one language of weights and measures will be spoken from the Equator to the Poles."

But in the next breath the Secretary of State was less as-suring. Whoever asked for any change was asking for trouble. And he gave fair warning to any legislator who would attempt to upset the people's "settled habits, their established usages, their ignorance, their prejudices."

A Time for Decision

Across the creaky floor of his office, the Secretary of State paced back and forth at four o'clock in the morning. John Quincy Adams was already at work, haunted by sleeplessness and his unfinished *Report to Congress on Weights and Measures*.

The problem was that Adams had no simple answer to give as to which system of measurements was better. He wavered, tormented by doubts. On the one hand the English system had its merits. On the other hand the metric system offered advantages. And yet, to come back to English measures . . . And so it went, pro and con. This was a man arguing with himself. The reply he was writing to a few questions from the House of Representatives had already become blown up into a full-sized book.

The Secretary of State was a portly, moon-faced little man whose eyes were constantly tearful from too much reading and whose fingers were cramped from too much writing. In his years as the United States minister to Russia Adams had spent the long winter nights reading the strange history of the world's measuring systems. Some men might have found the subject dull. But to Adams it was a fascinating study, and he became an amateur expert.

By the year 1820 America was no closer to a solution to the troublesome measurements question. People lined up on either side of the dispute between the old customary

English system and the new metric plan which came out of France.

A growing mood in the United States was to ignore the Old World altogether. The War of 1812 against England had left Americans with bitter memories. Napoleon was dying in exile, but he had turned all Europe into a smoldering battleground. With no taste for endless European wars and upheavals, plots and rivalries, many Americans simply turned their backs on the Continent.

As for those European nations that held possessions in the Western Hemisphere, the Secretary of State summed up United States policy in one sentence: "Keep what is yours, but leave the rest of this continent to us."

This nation was feeling its own young economic strength. For the time being, America chose to live between a high eastern wall of trade tariffs and a western frontier of boundless opportunities.

A majority of Americans were still on the farm. Isolated from the outside world at large, they traded locally and traveled little. They bought and sold close to home, relying on their wits not to get short weight or short measure in their dealings. But an increasing number of Americans felt the need for a universal, clear-cut system of weights and measures. Some looked to England, others to France.

American scientists were drawing closer to world science. In 1820 they were reading a brand-new magazine called *Silliman's Journal,* which brought home to them the latest research abroad in chemistry, astronomy, and physics. Gradually, scientists were being attracted to the metric system.

In these years of the American Industrial Revolution scientists were actively serving this country's manufacturers, applying their knowledge to the problems of engineering and invention. It was in this way that the metric system, or parts of it, found its way into the factory.

America had plunged into the world market with its manufactured goods. Rhode Island boasted of its teeming, smoky cotton mill towns. In Connecticut Eli Whitney's musket factory was producing by a new method of manufacture.

Whitney was a bachelor who spent every waking hour in his water- and steam-powered plant. With Whitney's innovations close measurement moved from the craftsman's workshop into the mass-production factory.

In that period of manufacture two nuts might fit the same bolt; but two triggers could rarely be interchanged in the same musket. However, Whitney discarded the old method of fitting part to part so that each was handmade and unique. Instead, his factory made musket parts that were standard in size and shape, uniform, and interchangeable. He was a brilliant inventor of power-driven machine tools, of instruments for exact measurement, of precision methods of mass production. In Whitney's factory a man could do a month's work in a day.

Lacking skilled workmen, America was eager for any means to save labor and time. And to John Quincy Adams America's old system of measurements seemed clumsy and wasteful. The Secretary of State saw in the metric system "the greatest invention since printing." He considered metric measurement a new power, greater than steam, the most useful of all "labor-saving machines!"

Yard or Meter?

In putting together his story of mankind and measurement, John Quincy Adams went back beyond old Noah and the Ark. Adams began his *Report to Congress on Weights and Measures* with the earliest man, "a solitary savage, ranging the forests."

From the very beginning man had a need for measuring units, most of which he found on his own body. By the time of the Flood, methods of measurement, the division of the day into units of time, the use of decimal numbers—all these had already been invented. Adams quoted the Old Testament warnings against the use of false measurements and fraudulent scales.

"You shall do no wrong in judgement, in measures of length or weight or quantity." Such was the word of the Lord. "You shall have just balances, just weights, a just *ephah,* and a just *hin.*" Adams was less concerned with *ephahs* and *hins* than he was with meters and yards.

On the Secretary of State's desk were piled the Bible, almanacs, the accounts of ancient Greece and Rome, the royal histories of Britain and France. However, all his vast learning on the subject hardly helped Adams to decide the knotty question at hand.

He was a bookish diplomat whose whole life was spent among top-ranking statesmen, noted scholars, and proper New England society. Soon to become the sixth president of the United States, Adams held the masses of Americans in both contempt and awe. Although he wanted earnestly to improve the measuring system of America, he was fearful about how the American people might respond to any change. Adams's report to Congress swung like a pendulum between two extremes.

Filled as it was with contradictory arguments, the report undoubtedly mirrored the confused state of public thinking about this whole matter. Faced with the problem of making a choice, the nation was simply deciding not to decide!

America was now being drawn into a lengthy war of words over measurement. The conflict would rage for a century and more. And Adams's report would furnish plenty of ammunition to both sides.

The loudest argument for the English system could be found on the docks of Boston, Philadelphia, and Charleston. The strongest commercial ties of the United States were still with England. Merchantmen unloaded British-made goods and carried away American cotton and tobacco, furs and grains. On all of them, the quantities, sizes, and weights were stamped in so-called English units.

Seaboard people involved in the commerce with England tended to favor English ways. The well-to-do bankers and merchants dressed in British woolens, sent their sons to school in England, stocked their homes with English furniture, cutlery, and china. And while most Americans figured in dollars, dimes, and cents, many of the wealthy still counted their profits in pounds, shillings, and pence.

Adoption of the metric system might be a step toward world unity, Adams declared in his scholarly report. But that move would certainly disrupt United States unity with England. Bitter rivals, England and France were not likely to agree on common measuring units.

To Adams it seemed strange how well nations managed to keep pace with each other in the instruments of war— "the same artillery and musketry, bayonets, swords and lances for the wholesale trade of human slaughter." Why should it be so difficult, he asked, to achieve world unity in the instruments of measurement which were to serve man's peaceful needs?

The United States federal government in those days had approved no official units of measurement. Some of the states had not acted officially on the matter. Many of the states owned measuring standards that were inaccurate, decayed, or worn with age. Most state laws referred to ancient standards locked away in English government buildings. Not many years passed before those standards went up in flames.

THE METER
FINDS
A HOME

On the blustery night of October 16, 1834, Charles Dickens awoke to cries of "Fire!" He was a young newspaper reporter, soon to become famous for his *Pickwick Papers* and later for his great novels of English life.

From the excitement in the streets it seemed as though all of London was burning. In reality, the fire was centered in the Houses of Parliament.

As the government buildings blazed in the high wind,

the newsman probed the causes of the fire. Some very old traditions, Dickens learned, had provided the kindling.

In the underground vaults of the Parliament palace were great piles of tallies. These were pieces of wood that had long been used as official receipts and accounts.

Wooden tallies, used in counting, numbering, measuring, have been known in every part of the world. Wooden sticks, with notches cut in them, recorded the transfer of goods and money. The tallies were split lengthwise so that the two parties to a business deal could hold matching halves.

The British, often slow to give up an outmoded custom, used tallies throughout the eighteenth century. But by 1834 the government at last decided to get rid of those heaps of rotting and worm-eaten wood.

"It would naturally occur to any intelligent person," wrote Charles Dickens, "that nothing could be easier than to allow them to be carried away for firewood by the miserable people who lived in that neighborhood.

"However, the order went out that they should be privately burned . . . in a stove in the House of Lords. The stove, over-gorged with these preposterous sticks, set fire to the panelling; the panelling set fire to the House of Commons; the two houses were reduced to ashes."

The reporter discovered that the flames had also destroyed the standards of measurement used by most of the English-speaking world. The yard and the gallon, the pound and the bushel—these were represented by official models that were stored in the vaults of Parliament. In the fire of 1834 all became a pile of cinders.

These standards were rather old, poorly made and inaccurate. An expert in the science of measurement reported that the three-hundred-year-old British standard for the yard was no better than "a common kitchen poker, filed at the ends by the most bungling workman."

This iron standard was supposed to have been based on the arm length of Queen Elizabeth I, who ruled England in the sixteenth century. Sometime during the years between, the metal rod had been broken apart and the pieces loosely joined together. A container that was supposed to represent the bushel had been around for so long that no one knew its true age or origin.

Although they were long used as standards by many nations, the so-called English weights and measures were really relics from the dim past. They were constantly being tested in the courts of law and found wanting. The British courtrooms were crowded with cases involving buyers and sellers who claimed that they were being cheated through misuse of the measuring system. Such cases became known as "assizes." In the London courts justice often depended on measuring goods in comparison with crumbling and moldering official standards.

Following the disastrous 1834 fire, scientists tried to put together the remains of the charred British standards. Poking among the ashes, they found little. They made copies of copies stored in other countries that used English measurements.

The new vaults in London were built to last, safeguarded from fire and theft and natural disasters. But somehow the British standards were never again considered to be quite so trustworthy.

The Parliament fire set many nations searching for universal and dependable standards. Some, including the United States, suddenly began to see the metric system in a new light.

A New Science

The meter had been born in France. But for forty years it remained a sort of stepchild.

Most French people continued to use two measuring systems, the old and the new. Peasants and shopkeepers balked at change. Statesmen wavered in their support. The scientists of France believed in the metric plan, but they seemed to have little influence on the rest of the country.

New Year's Day 1840 changed all that. On that morning the metric system became the law of the land. Any French merchant or farmer or tradesman using another system was subject to arrest. The law was tough, imposing a fine of ten to twenty francs for each offense. Instead of two systems France now had one.

If there was a single shout of joy that day, perhaps it came from the French school children. They could soon scrap those troublesome conversion tables. Anyone living in a country using two measuring systems needed to know both the old and the new—and also how to translate one into the other. Many a tiresome school day was spent in endless drilling on the tables of equivalents. Conversion was a matter of memorizing long lists of figures, a task that the school children would be happy to forget.

As rival nations, France and Germany were seldom able to agree on anything. But in the mid-eighteenth century the metric system came to Germany. The new units were first adopted piecemeal by parts of Germany, but in time the entire nation went over to metric usage. Trading in goods was growing livelier across the boundaries of Europe. And people speaking many languages came to reckon the value of cheese and wine, fabric and coal in metric terms.

The official metric system crossed the Atlantic in 1850.

The first country in the Western Hemisphere to adopt the complete new method was Colombia.

In New England industry and commerce were booming. The day of the fast, graceful, full-sailed clipper ship had arrived. And from the northern seaports of the United States, the Yankee clippers were carrying manufactured goods abroad. The smooth-curved sailing vessels raced across the Atlantic with their holds full of American-made sewing machines, clocks, printing presses, and machine tools.

Designers in the United States had perfected power-driven lathes and milling machines used for the precise shaping and cutting of metals. French and German firms imported the expensive but finely built American machines. Even the British, first in industry, copied Yankee models.

It was the Americans who excelled in designing measuring instruments and gauges for factory use. With a rising interest in exact measurement, many American manufacturers took a favorable view of the metric system.

Connecticut, its river towns and seaports thriving, seemed to sense a future trend. The state took an important new step. As part of their arithmetic, children in the Connecticut schools were taught the metric system.

Arithmetic is a word that expresses an ancient Greek idea—the "art of measuring," based on the personal skills of artisans. Once considered an art, measuring in the 1850s had become a science. A new word was being heard more and more—metrology, the science of measurement. And in the scientific laboratory increased study and research centered in this new field. Modern science was relying more and more on fine measurement and the use of a wide variety of new measuring instruments.

Fifty leading American scientists gathered in the Capitol on a rainy autumn day in 1863. The nation was in the grip of Civil War. But Congress had chosen this stormy time in which to establish the National Academy of Sciences.

In its opening session, the first committee set up by the scientists was one to deal with "the uniformity of weights and measures." For its chairman they chose the physicist Joseph Henry.

Law of the Land

A horse-drawn coach clattered northward through the dark streets of Washington, D. C., on a warm July night. At front and rear were cavalry escorts. The contents of the coach had been carefully packed by a small group of scientists. Joseph Henry among them.

In the cargo were the measurement standards of the United States government—including those for the yard and the pound, but also for the meter and the kilogram. The convoy was headed toward a secret hiding place in Vermont. Embattled Washington was no longer a safe location for such important items.

The summer of 1864 found the capital withered by drought and disheartened by the long and grim war. Confederate General Jubal Early was marching on Washington from the Shenandoah hills. And when Joseph Henry reached home just before dawn, he could hear cannon booming to the west.

The scientist walked briskly toward the strange castle in which he lived. He was Secretary of the Smithsonian Institution. With his family, he resided in this many-turreted, red-brick structure set on a vast meadow, later called the Mall. The huge building stood midway between the half-built, temporarily abandoned Washington Monument and the Capitol, with its dome still unfinished.

Henry had hoped to make the Smithsonian Institution a center for original scientific research. But its halls were already cluttered with curiosities, dusty mementos of the past and historical relics, the working models of American inventors and exotic gifts to presidents of the United States from foreign monarchs. One day it would be called "the attic of the nation."

Henry was a physicist at the peak of a brilliant scientific career. Bold as he was in his experiments with electromagnets, he was a cautious man outside the laboratory, sober and hard-working. Other men became famous and wealthy with inventions based on Henry's research. But the physicist remained loyal to the cause of pure science.

A good part of his time was given in those days to the problem of weights and measures. To a man, his committee of leading American scientists was in favor of one universal system for all the world.

In January 1866 Henry presented to Congress the view of the nation's leading scientists. "In their opinion," he reported, "the metrical system of weights and measures, though not without defects, is the best in use." Careful to point to the difficulties of changing to a new system, he urged that the new units be first taught in the nation's schools, that the change should be "the work of time and through the education of the rising generation."

Six months passed. On July 28, 1866, a messenger from the Capitol brought President Andrew Johnson an approved bill which he signed. This was the first time the words "metric system" had ever appeared in America's laws.

The Meter Is Legal

The 1866 law was a curious one. It said nothing about what the American people *should* do. It did say what they *could* do.

It was now lawful in the United States "to employ the weights and measures of the metric system." The law settled nothing. A merchant could sell muslin by the meter and jars of jam by the kilogram—if he wanted to—without being thrown in jail.

Many Americans saw the law as a step in a new direction. The United States now became a party to a world-wide agreement that the metric system would be used in the handling of international mail. Postal authorities agreed on a single world standard rate for letters weighing no more than fifteen grams. The 1866 metric law encouraged scientists, map makers, engineers, instrument makers, and government officials to participate in international meetings dealing with measurement.

As Joseph Henry saw it, the new law meant much to America's scientific community. The number of scientists serving the United States government was increasing year by year. Many were involved in testing products purchased by the government, making maps, recording weather conditions, dealing with public health problems, advising officials on natural resources. Scientists were now free to use the metric system wherever it was practical. More important, American scientists were now better able to keep in touch with the work of European scientists, most of whom were already using metric measurements.

Henry was in the very center of international scientific activity. At the Smithsonian he set up a global Exchange Service to be used by scientists throughout the world. A lively flow of scientific information, specimens, instruments, apparatus went back and forth between American scientists and those overseas.

"The worth and importance of the Institution," Henry said about the Smithsonian, "are not to be estimated by what it accumulates within the walls of its building, but by what it sends forth to the world."

The world of the 1870s had indeed become science-minded. A continuous train of new knowledge linked scientists with inventors and engineers, with the leaders of industry and commerce. Nowhere was this more evident than in the new field of electricity, which was transforming basic scientific research into power stations and motors, electrical servants for the people and brilliant lights. Uniform measurement was more important than ever—and not only in terms of common units for length, time, mass, temperature. The electrical age was making its demand for standardized units of electric current, resistance, inductance.

It was Joseph Henry the physicist who had done outstanding research in electric inductance. His discoveries revealed how a current in one electrical circuit produces a magnetic field—which in turn induces a current in another nearby circuit.

In later years a new unit would be added to the metric system and used throughout the world for measuring the effect of a varying electric current. This unit would be named the "henry," in honor of the American physicist.

In September 1872 Henry was on his way to Europe. He was an official delegate of the United States to a conference of thirty nations on metric measurement.

As yet, no world center had been established by the countries using the metric system. Joseph Henry was among those who found the meter a home.

NATURE
SETS A
STANDARD

Out of a revolution that swept away the old and corrupt monarchy of France came the metric system.

What could be a more fitting location for the world metric headquarters than a majestic palace, one of the many once owned by the French nobility?

A former royal residence, the Pavillon de Breteuil stood, surrounded by a large park in a Paris suburb. The French government gave this palace in Sèvres to the world, to be used as headquarters for the International Bureau of Weights and Measures.

Seventeen nations were the first signers of the 1875 Treaty of the Meter, which established the global organization. Although it was not a metric nation, the United States signed the treaty after it was approved by Congress.

The bureau at Sèvres was charged with safeguarding the standards of the metric system, building a great laboratory of metrology, comparing the standards used by the member nations with the international prototypes regularly and often, holding a meeting every six years to consider new developments. At their meeting in France the delegates were keenly aware that the world to be measured was a fast-changing one.

All of France in the 1870s seemed to be reading a novel by a writer named Jules Verne. *Around the World in Eighty Days* was the story of a daring wager made by a young Englishman that he could reduce the size of the globe to eighty days of travel time. The hero of this exciting adventure won the bet.

Verne's book dramatized the fact that the world had become smaller because of speedy travel and telegraphic communication. Even old-fashioned methods of measuring distance no longer seemed sensible. Once, distance had been reckoned by many peoples, including American Indians, in terms of days of travel. But a single day's journey now took on a new meaning.

Jules Verne's popular book on man's newly found ability to travel far and fast was very much in the mood of the times. A gas-filled balloon riding swift wind currents could carry passengers over land and sea, across natural barriers and national boundaries. Somehow it now seemed odder than ever that nations would cling to their separate ways of measuring distance.

This was a time for bold feats of technology and engineering. There was much talk in those years about a tunnel across the English Channel. The French reckoned the distance as fifty-four kilometers, the English as thirty-four miles.

People wondered what might happen if the British began tunneling at one end according to a plan based on inches and pounds—while the French used meters and kilograms? Would the two ever meet?

The trends of the times linked peoples more closely together. Trade and travel, education and science, technology and industry—all were spreading beyond the borders of nations. All were hampered by the differences in measuring units: Two systems were at odds with each other.

Railroads across Europe ran head-on into the problems of inch-pound versus meter-kilogram. English parts could not be used on French bicycles and vice versa. The French wrench did not fit the British bolt.

A cable had been laid across the Atlantic Ocean, linking the hemispheres by telegraph. Europe seemed to be listening for the message from overseas. Did America perhaps have a word of peace that would help settle Europe's war of measurements?

Tug of War

As the United States began its second century in 1876, it was not really within the world family of metric nations. Nor was it completely out.

The metric question had become a tug of war. A growing body of people in the United States were pushing hard toward a metric America. An organized force of similar strength was pulling the other way. In Congress and out opinions clashed. As the years ran on, people took sides in the market places, the courthouses, the workshops, the laboratories. In shrill tones the nation battled over the foot and the meter. For every argument favoring the metric system, there was sure to be one against.

"The change to metric will drive us to ruin," shouted one group of businessmen. "American trade is dying by inches!" replied those opposed to the inch-pound system.

"Every child will save a year in school once we go to a decimal system," was an argument commonly heard.

"If we really need a decimal system," was the comeback, "let's decimalize the inch!"

Even race and religion were dragged into the mounting dispute. Inches and pounds were God's gift to the "superior Anglo-Saxon race," it was claimed by those who also charged that the metric system was invented "in a godless revolution by an inferior people."

In Boston a group of metric enthusiasts sent out loads of material describing the system, as well as school kits with meter sticks, wall charts, iron weights, containers, and tape measures in metric units.

In the same city a group of men formed what they called the International Institute for Preserving and Perfecting the Anglo-Saxon Weights and Measures. They claimed that the inch and the foot had been used and handed down by the builders of the Egyptian pyramids, acting under divine guidance.

The so-called International Institute objected to the Statue of Liberty, which was then being constructed as a gift to America by the French people. "There is one thing we do not like about the statue," complained the antimetric group, "We prefer a statue of liberty measured in good Anglo-Saxon inches, not in French millimeters."

Supporters strongly denied that the changeover to metric measurement in the United States would be difficult or that it would cost more than it was worth. "Our money is already decimal," they said, "the rest will be as easy as counting to ten."

"We can't stop America's progress," argued the metric opponents, "while this country learns how to count in a foreign language."

The opposition also pointed out that the metric system was now legal in the United States "Let those who want to use it do so," they declared, "and leave the rest of us alone."

However, many Americans feared that their country would be left behind while the metric system was being adopted by the so-called enlightened nations of the world.

Fixing the Size

In 1896 a fleet-footed young American named Thomas Burke sprinted his way to fame. He became the winner of two track championships at the first modern Olympic Games, held in Athens, Greece. Sports enthusiasts in America became acquainted with the metric system as Burke won the 100-meter run and then the 400-meter run.

By this time the greater part of Europe was already on the metric system. The one important holdout was Great Britain. Members of Parliament wrangled at great length over the merits of the two rival systems of measurement.

The debates ended with the decision of the British Empire to keep its vast array of the old customary units, eliminating a few for simplicity, changing some for more clarity.

Meanwhile, virtually all of Latin America, from Mexico to the tip of Argentina, had switched to the metric system. A market of growing importance in the world, the South American continent was now being measured in kilometers, its produce sold in kilograms.

Measurements were becoming more and more precise. Science, technology, manufacturing were using increasingly fine gradations of size and mass. No modern nation could rely any longer on old standards locked away in a vault. Such standards needed periodic checking to detect the slightest change. Metrology now required a very complete central laboratory, equipped with the most sensitive instruments man could devise. For nations on the English system, no such scientific resources were available. The international metric headquarters in France had become the foremost center of metrology in the world.

American officials mulled over these problems for a long time. Then on April 5, 1893, came a far-reaching government decision.

"The Office of Weights and Measures will in the future regard the International Prototype *Meter* and *Kilogram* as fundamental standards." The meaning of this announcement from the United States Department of the Treasury was that the metric system now became the legal source of reference for all official United States measurements.

Americans were free to continue using the inch and pound. But these units were firmly pegged to the international meter and kilogram on the basis of a set ratio. It was no longer Washington or London but the metric palace in

Sèvres, France, which now held the key to United States measurements.

There remained in Washington, a platinum-uranium bar on which two lines had been engraved to duplicate the length of the meter standard in France. But this bar, representing a set number of inches, had to be taken periodically to the international metric headquarters in France to be checked and verified. On every trip it made to be measured the bar had changed slightly in size.

The science of metrology was rapidly outgrowing the use of metal standards, no matter how skillfully made. Two extremely fine scratches on a platinum bar might indicate the span of one meter. But the scratches were no longer fine enough, nor was the metal resistant enough to change. The world needed a precise standard of length which could not be damaged or destroyed, perferably a standard "taken from nature" that could be duplicated by any nation.

The world's measurement experts pondered that problem. An American out of the "Wild West" solved it for them.

Measurer of Light

A tall, slender lad of sixteen shook the dust of Nevada from his clothes on a June day in 1869. Albert A. Michelson had come East for a career in science.

Almost forty years were to pass before Michelson would become the first American scientist to win a Nobel Prize. The physicist was to be honored for the methods which he discovered "for the exactness of measurements."

However, the four decades between were to be filled

with hard work and brilliant new insights. Michelson, whose boyhood was spent in the rough, boisterous mining camps of the American frontier, was soon to become famous throughout the world as "the measurer of light." His career as a scientist would also be intertwined with the development of the metric system.

As early as Galileo's time, scientists had tried to determine the speed of light. When Michelson began his research, the only measurements that had been made were approximate, and the methods used were rather crude.

In the year 1882 Michelson developed his own apparatus and instruments, repeating his experiments scores of times before he was satisfied that he had a precise new measurement for the velocity of light. He announced it as 299,583 kilometers per second. That remained the accepted figure for the next half century. And when further research led to a more accurate measurement, it was Michelson who made the change.

Among scientists the metric system had become universal. Michelson used it in his work. But the physicist also became deeply interested in the science of metrology. He returned to an old problem—matching the meter with some natural standard.

The meter had turned out to be only as long as itself, with no known twin in nature. Scientists had discarded the relation between the meter and the earth's circumference. The meter was not one ten-millionth of the quadrant as had been assumed.

It seemed too late to try to change the size of the meter. And no natural object or phenomenon had as yet been found which corresponded exactly to the length that had been chosen for the meter. However, it did seem possible to select something unchangeable in nature which in a given quantity would equal the meter's fixed dimension.

To Michelson and a number of his fellow scientists, it appeared that the solution to the problem lay in light waves. The American physicist turned to a deeper study of a variety of light sources and the waves which are emitted.

A beam of light, which may appear as a straight line, is in reality a continuous train of tiny waves. Chemical elements, heated to luminous intensity, give off light in characteristic wavelengths.

Michelson went to work at answering a challenging question: why not define the meter in terms of wavelengths?

A Match for the Meter

In the summer of 1892 Michelson was hard at work in France. The scientist had been invited to the international metric center to carry on his effort to find a new fixed standard for the meter. The bar of metal was giving way to a wavelength of light.

Michelson displayed experiments with his interferometer, an instrument using mirrors to split a light beam from a single source and to reflect back the two component beams. The Michelson interferometer was capable of measuring differences in length as small as the wavelength of light. It would take more than a million and a half such wavelengths to equal the distance of one meter.

A gentle and modest man, Michelson astonished his European fellow scientists with his exceedingly fine measurements. The American had carried metrology to new heights. His experiments in fixing the speed of the earth through space and in measuring the size of stars were known world-wide. He had measured variations in the influences of the sun and the moon on tides.

Through his year of work in France Michelson established the wavelength as the basis for a practical standard for the meter. The physicist began a search for a suitable chemical element as a light source, with a clearly defined line in its spectrum. He worked with the element sodium. He then found a better line for measurement in the vivid green band of mercury. Eventually, he was attracted to the bright red line of cadmium.

The hunt for the most suitable element would continue for many years. While Michelson worked in the Paris suburb, a group of British chemists in London were in the act of discovering krypton, the element which was later to become the wavelength basis for the metric standard.

Would a wavelength standard for the meter remain fixed forever? Michelson answered the question with the scientist's clear understanding that nothing in the universe is changeless.

"In the course of millions of years the properties of the atoms which emit these radiations may change," said the physicist. With a shy grin, he added "But probably by that time the human race will have lost interest in this problem."

A long quest was ending. Mankind had suddenly outgrown measurements that were once defined in terms of a king's waistline, that were as changeable as his eating habits. Units of length, originally based on the size of an arm, a barleycorn, a human foot, seemed ludicrously obsolete. Moreover, the world need not rely on a man-made piece of metal, subject to the subtle erosions of time. Michelson had made it possible for the fixed meter to be duplicated ex-

actly in a scientific laboratory in any part of the world—or
even in outer space!

Michelson, the genius of refined measurement, the creator of precision instruments and experiments, worked
among a group of bright assistants. One of them was a
young specialist in measurement named Samuel W. Stratton.

THE GLOBE
TURNS
METRIC

D<small>r.</small> Samuel W. Stratton came to Washington, D. C., on the strength of a promise. How could any scientist ignore a chance for a superb new laboratory of his own?

A bachelor in his late thirties, Stratton said good-by to Michelson and to the research they were doing together at the University of Chicago. The physicist arrived in the capital in the year 1900. He was to become head of a brand-new agency of the government, the National Bureau of Standards.

Turn-of-the-century America was certainly lacking in certain standards. It was a time of confusion—when even time was confusing. There was still no law regulating standard time zones across the country.

In the Chicago Board of Trade millions of bushels of corn, wheat, rye changed hands every day—but there was no single agreed size for the bushel.

In Philadelphia giant locomotives were being manufactured. Their wheels were made to fit tracks laid 4 feet 8.5 inches apart—but thousands of miles of railroad had been built to entirely different gauges.

Baseball was the national game—but it would be years before the distance between home plate and the pitcher's mound would be standardized at 60.6 feet.

Electrical power was flowing from the new dynamos at Niagara Falls, but there was still no universal agreement on the measuring of electrical energy. A new word—kilowatt, meaning a thousand watts—was just coming into use.

In those years there were no standard widths or thicknesses for lumber. Pipes and fittings came in a bewildering range of sizes. The journeyman bricklayer could not journey very far before finding local kilns producing brick in unfamiliar dimensions.

Stratton waited a year in Washington before his new agency could be established by Congress. But he lost no time in planning the laboratory of the National Bureau of Standards, which would not only set uniform standards for many areas of American life, but would also do important research in chemistry, physics, mathematics, and engineering.

However, the new bureau chief was immediately faced with a knotty problem. New official standards were to be set up in many fields. Should they be fixed in terms of the old customary units of inches and pounds? Or was America ready to move on to the metric system?

Perhaps he was expected to be impartial in this matter. But Stratton found it very difficult to hide the fact that he believed strongly in metric measurement.

A recent Congress had almost given its endorsement to the metric system. The bill lost by two votes. Congressmen were ready to try again.

The New York Times, although opposed to the meter, admitted glumly that it would soon be adopted. A Milwaukee newspaper predicted metric approval: "It is as sure as anything in the future can be sure." To Stratton, it seemed that a metric America was near at hand. The notion was widely shared.

Stratton had grown up on the Illinois prairie. He learned farming but also mechanics, working with farm machinery. Stratton went on to become a mechnical engineer. In time he moved into the scientific world by way of physics and electrical engineering.

He was a sturdily built man with a dark mop of hair and a heavy mustache. In a deep, resounding voice, he spoke with authority on the wide range of matters that came before his bureau. Stratton knew first hand about America's need for clear, uniform, and universal standards. What he did not know was the strange workings of politics in the nation's capital.

A small but well-financed office had been opened in Washington. Its business was to block the metric bill at all costs. It was the kind of organization that in later years would be called a lobby. Its paid officials had the task of visiting Congressmen privately and influencing their vote by one means or another.

To Stratton's amazement the strong prometric sentiment in Congress suddenly began to shift. One metric bill failed to pass by a narrow margin, and then another by a wider gap.

"The opponents of the metric system see to it that every Congressman is reached"—Stratton complained to a friend —"and Congress does not see that it originates practically from a single source."

The antimetric lobby had the backing of powerful American manufacturing companies. The arguments they used were not original but were somehow very persuasive. They painted a picture of an America thrown into total disorder and discord if the metric bill became law. This country, the metric foes said, already had the best of all possible measuring systems. "The inch will never die," they vowed.

The antimetric campaigners posed as protectors of America against some kind of "foreign invasion." They warned of grave dangers to the nation's working men and women, and they pleaded that the meter was a menace to school children. Metric advocates like Stratton were denounced as enemies of America, trying to force an alien way of life on the common people.

In calm and reasoned testimony before Congress Stratton said that he believed that in a short time people could learn to think in the new system. "We must give all classes of people the credit for having a certain amount of intelligence and common sense," he declared.

The National Bureau of Standards became a storm center. Around it swirled the furious winds of the metric controversy. Stratton, vexed and discouraged, became the target for personal attacks. For the time being the metric battle was running downhill.

In one last effort Stratton asked for the help of an old friend. A telephone call brought Alexander Graham Bell to the Capitol.

"The Men Like It"

On a rocky gulf in Nova Scotia, Alexander Graham Bell was absorbed in the world of flight. The creator of the telephone had moved on to another kind of invention which would further serve to make the earth smaller.

The flying machines which Bell now designed were complicated versions of the box kite. He and his assistants built them in a large shed near his Nova Scotia summer home. A huge red silk box would sometimes flutter briefly over the beach. Often the pilot got himself a ducking in the cold waters of the bay.

The future of flying had already been assured a few years earlier by the Wright brothers and their successful powered flight at Kitty Hawk, North Carolina. But Bell had some ideas of his own about aircraft which he wanted to develop. His telephone had already founded a prosperous industry. And Bell now spent the late years of his life in other creative ventures.

It was in his research on aviation that Bell first stumbled on the idea of using the metric system. His designs involved an immense amount of calculation. Bell spent weeks figuring out the ratios between the lifting surfaces and the total mass of the aircraft.

"The calculations proved to be so laborious," he later recalled, "that I found it simpler to translate the proposed measurements into metrical terms and then work out the solution on the metrical plan."

Bell employed ordinary workmen, carpenters, mechanics in his workshop. To his delight he found that they had no trouble understanding his drawings and instructions, once the metric system was explained.

"So long as I did not ask my men to translate from one system into the other, all was plain sailing," he recounted. The inventor had found a key to an easier method of work. "And the men like it!" he added.

On February 16, 1906, Bell came before a committee of the House of Representatives to tell of his experiences with the metric system. He was a striking figure, a man of sixty, world famous. His tanned skin and dark eyes were set off by a spray of snowy whiskers. Bell spoke in a clear, melodic voice and the congressmen became rapt in his words.

The inventor began by talking about the American coal miner and his problems with the long ton and the short ton. In order to get paid for mining a ton of coal the miner had to produce 2240 pounds. However, when he bought a ton of coal to heat his home, the miner received only 2000 pounds.

"In a similar manner, we have different kinds of bushels and gallons and other measures in common use; and if there is anything that is clear, it seems to be this," said Bell, "we need uniformity in our weights and measures."

Speaking as a man experienced in industry, Bell shattered the argument that the adoption of metric measurements would mean the scrapping of expensive machinery.

"A tool or machine has only a limited life," declared Bell. "It may last, say, ten years, and then it must be replaced." Since the change to the metric system would be a gradual matter taking place perhaps over a ten-year period, such equipment could be naturally retired with little loss.

The antimetric lobby had long scoffed at the meter's main supporters as men without practical knowledge in the world of business and industry. But Alexander Graham Bell was the living challenge to that notion. His very name was a symbol for success in technology.

"The metrical system is the only system known that has a ghost of a chance of being adopted universally," Bell said in the Capitol committee room.

The Congressmen had also heard from Stratton that "there is not the slightest possibility of our own system, full of inconsistent ratios, inelastic and unsuitable for many purposes, with the same name for different units, ever becoming universal."

In those years Great Britain and the United States seemed to be in a race as to which of the two countries would first adopt the metric system, with the other following soon after. "Shall we not take the lead?" asked Stratton. Both Stratton and Bell made it clear that the longer America waited, the more difficult it would be to change.

Only chaos could result, Bell told Congress, if each individual decided to use his own system of measurements or if each community or state in the Union did so. In the same way, said the inventor, it was wrong for the United States to use "a peculiar system of its own, without reference to the usages of other countries, as if we formed an isolated people having no dealings with the rest of the world."

And yet, that was exactly what America was to continue doing for the next sixty years.

Inching Along

The poor progress of the meter in the United States was not a good measure of the nation's progress in the early twentieth century.

New towers pierced the skies and great cities grew. America's streets and roads filled with motor cars. Humming wires carried a surge of electrical power to the most remote farmstead.

The defenders of the meter stumbled with every stride forward. Their cause never became popular. They remained in the 1920s a small, zealous group, engaged in an uphill battle.

In congressional hearings they were described as "fanatics," "foreigners," and "radicals." Supporters of the metric system were labeled "metricites," as though they were dangerous bugs!

The opposition kept them busy with running attacks. During one brief period in 1920 the newspapers were filled with "a metric plot." The mastermind was supposedly "Mr. Z—a secret German agent with a scar on his forehead." "Mr. Z" actually turned out to be a prosperous San Francisco businessman, who did contribute money to the pro-metric cause but preferred to remain in the background.

The foes of the meter constantly came up with new tales of the "failure" of the metric system in other lands. Rice was not weighed by the kilogram in Asian countries, they said. Mexican railroads were not being run on a metric plan. And even France, the home of the meter, was buying British steel by the ton.

The active antimetric lobby in Washington spread the idea that the meter was the plaything of fuzzy-minded professors and impractical dreamers. One letter sent to the editors of numerous newspapers was entitled, "What Real He-Men Think of the Compulsory Metric System"—very little, of course.

The main weapon against the meter was fear. People were led to believe that a change to metric measurement would upset the deeds to their real estate, the recipes in cookbooks, the length of a football field, the cost of groceries, the fit of clothing. Americans were frightened with visions of business bankruptcies, loss of jobs, a long period of uncertainty and upheaval.

There was plenty of evidence to prove that none of this was likely. No other country had experienced such crises in changing to the metric system. But the myth of a metric monster had been set loose in this land, and it could no longer be easily dispelled.

Two world wars pushed the American argument about the meter into the background. Between the wars came a long period of isolationism, in which the nation turned a wary eye on anything that smacked of foreign influence or international cooperation. During the long Depression America had other pressing matters to think about.

Meanwhile, the world's metric balance was shifting. Two of the most populous nations in the world, the Soviet Union and later China, changed to the metric system. The years following World War II saw a steady swing of nations to the banner of the meter.

In the United States industries producing pharmaceuticals and optical appliances, radio and electronic equipment, were using metric units. Leaders in the grocery business spoke out for the metric system as a way of simplifying the sizes of cans and packages.

But no single bill favoring metric measurement got very far in Congress. "Don't give an inch!" was the slogan of the antimetric lobby. The American automobile industry had developed a new model in measures—the decimal inch.

According to the motor car makers their unit combined the best of both worlds. Industry could continue using the familiar inch. At the same time the new measurements added all the obvious advantages of decimals. Under this scheme the inch was divided not into halves, quarters, eighths, and sixteenths, but into ten parts, a hundred parts, a thousand parts.

The decimal inch was not really a substitute for the metric system since it dealt only with the problem of small units of length. Instead of solving America's fundamental problem of a universal system of measurements, the new method seemed to add a new complication, being neither "English" nor metric.

Nevertheless, the decimal inch served for purposes of shop work in doing away with unwieldy fractions. The thousandth of an inch became the new unit of measure in many metal-working industries.

As America moved past mid-century, the trend was toward more "scientific" methods of producing goods. Workmen became highly skilled in dealing with close tolerances, cutting and shaping materials to precise specified sizes. Fine measurement in the factory was governed by what became known as quality control. Automation added another dimension of exactness. The electronic computer took over the control of many fine gauging, inspecting, and measuring tasks.

The manufacturer depended more and more on the engineer. In turn the engineer worked more closely with the scientist. As for the scientist, his language of measurement throughout the world was the metric system.

On October 4, 1957, a radio announcement from Moscow explained a glittering object that had suddenly appeared in the sky. This first space satellite, announced the Russians, was "in orbit 900 kilometers from the earth, 58 centimeters in diameter, with a mass of 83.6 kilograms." Sputnik heralded the Space Age—and a metric world.

America Stands Alone

At the dawn of modern science, almost four centuries ago, a few letters passed across the Alps between Kepler, the German astronomer, and Galileo, a fellow scientist in Italy. Those letters were early forerunners to today's international scientific cooperation.

In the summer of 1957 sixty thousand scientists from sixty-six nations joined in a wide range of common activity. This was IGY, the International Geophysical Year. The participants spoke in many tongues. But the language of measurement was metric.

The launching of Sputnik was only one of the many brilliant highlights of the IGY. Scientists discovered and mapped new ocean currents. They collected new data on the movements of glaciers in the Alps. Projects were launched that burrowed into the earth's interior. An entire continent, Antarctica, was marked out as an international scientific laboratory.

Space research was begun that was to land man on the moon. One IGY project centered its attention on a little-known portion of the earth, the Indian Ocean. Out of the research came the plan for a submarine voyage under the

Arctic ice. Scientists joined in studying the global changes in the air that shape the weather patterns of every region.

Much of the work centered on simultaneous measurements taken from many points on the earth's surface. From far-flung stations a picture of the globe at one given moment in time was pieced together, including data on weather, upper air movements, ocean conditions, the earth's magnetic field, influences of the sun. The IGY compiled an enormous quantity of metric data, available to all nations, the largest and the oldest, the small ones and those newly formed.

In Guinea, toward the end of the IGY, a few research scientists and students, laden with instruments, climbed the towering highlands which crown their country. The people of Guinea had only within recent weeks declared themselves an independent nation, among the first in black Africa to end the centuries of colonial rule. One of the first acts of the young republic was to adopt the metric system.

In quick succession Guinea was followed by other rapidly emerging countries of Africa. Across the entire continent nation after nation swung over to the metric system.

The year 1962 saw the metric system in use throughout Asia, from Korea and India to Asia Minor. In that year Japan ended its uneasy shifting back and forth between the metric and its customary systems of measurement. For half a century, Japan lived with three legal measuring systems —metric, inch-pound, and *shaku-kan,* the ancient Japanese system of units.

In the 1920s Japan had tried to limit itself to metric usage. But the government backed down before the outcries that metric was foreign, the complaints that the change would be costly, and the fears that the growing Japanese economy would be upset. In the 1950s Japan tried again, this time taking a firmer stand for metric units. By 1962 the country could report success. A strict law imposed a fine amounting to $140 on anyone who used a system other than metric—but not one violation of the law was reported!

Among the big powers of the world the United States was now left with a single inch-pound ally—Great Britain. But on May 24, 1965, the bell announcing the opening of Parliament tolled the end of the English system of measurements in Great Britain. That morning the president of the Board of Trade proposed that "British industries adopt metric units until that system can become in time the primary system for the country as a whole." Britain soon began a ten-year metric conversion, to be completed in 1975.

Suddenly, the United States was finding itself alone in a metric world. Australia and New Zealand had joined the march to metric measurement. With Canada committed to the metric system, the United States confronted the meter across every border and in every nation with which it had dealings of any importance. Outside the United States 99 per cent of the world's people were committing themselves to measuring in meters. Only thirteen countries were still holding out against the metric system—Barbados, Burma, Gambia, Ghana, Jamaica, Liberia, Muscat and Oman, Nauru, Sierra Leone, Southern Yemen, Tonga, Trinidad —and the United States!

In 1968 Congress called upon the National Bureau of Standards, now in the Department of Commerce, to conduct a thorough study of the problem. Over three years the Bureau probed every aspect of the question, reviewed the advantages and disadvantages, the experiences of other nations, the views of American consumers, business people, workers, educators. In 1971 the United States Metric Study was complete, showing clearly that America was moving steadily toward more and more metric usage.

The recommendations of the report were summed up in the words of Maurice H. Stans, Secretary of Commerce.

—That the United States change to the International Metric System deliberately and carefully;

—That early priority be given to educating every American school child and the public at large to think in metric terms;

—That the Congress, after deciding on a plan for the nation, establish a target date ten years ahead, by which time the U. S. will have become predominantly, though not exclusively, metric;

—That there be a firm government commitment to this goal.

A UNITY
OF UNITS

America's journey from the foot to the meter may be a long one. But this nation is already part of the way there.

Far from being foreign to America, metric units may be found in daily use in the school, the sports arena, the hospital, the factory, the scientific laboratory, and even the home.

Hassler, Henry, Michelson—these and many other Americans made important contributions to the development of the international metric system. For more than a century metric standards have been the only ones that were legal in the United States, the only units ever formally approved by Congress.

Today's official and legal United States standards are all metric, maintained by the National Bureau of Standards at Gaithersburg, Maryland. Americans still measure length by feet and yards; area is figured in terms of acres; volume is reckoned in bushels and pecks. However, by law, the American reference standard for all three measurements is the meter.

The medicine cabinet and the pantry shelves in the American home are now full of metric units. Vitamins are dispensed in milligrams and prescriptions are compounded in metric quantities. Many spices and cake mixes are packaged in metric amounts.

United States athletes compete for Olympic medals. In track, swimming, skating, and many other sports, the official distances are in meters.

The metric system has been adopted by United States producers of roller bearings, photographic film, skis, electronic equipment, spark plugs, optical devices, electrical power. Several years ago the Ford Motor Company designed the Pinto, the first American automobile with motor and transmission parts in metric sizes. A new automobile plant in Lima, Ohio, builds engines with metric measurements.

In the Alabama city of Huntsville signs on the streets tell how fast a car may go—in both miles and kilometers per hour. In a large complex of government buildings, the thermometers give the room temperatures in degrees Celsius. This is the Huntsville headquarters of the National Aeronautics and Space Administration.

Back in 1970 NASA began going metric. Its scientific and technical publications changed to the use of metric units. By 1973 all of NASA's reports to Congress were being written in metric terms.

The space agency deals with a large segment of American business as a buyer of equipment and services. Based on its research and development work, NASA also issues valuable reports to industry. All this information is now being expressed in metric language.

Metric terms are familiar to thousands of American children who are taught the system in school. The pupil quickly learns how simply metric units are related to each other and to our counting system of tens.

In measuring length according to the old "English" system, the units increase by an uneven series of steps. Divide the number of inches *by 12* to get the number of feet; divide feet *by 3* to get yards; divide yards *by 5½* to get rods; divide rods *by 40* to get furlongs; divide furlongs *by 8* to get miles.

However, in the metric system, the units of length increase or decrease by a factor of 10; or by 10×10; or by $10 \times 10 \times 10$. And so on. The up and down steps of metric units are tens, corresponding to the decimal system of numbers familiar to America and all the world. Every metric unit may be divided into ten equal parts, each part being the next lower unit in the scale.

Much of the metric language is already well known to Americans. The terms used when units are raised or lowered in quantity or value are based on a set of prefixes. For example, the base unit of length, the meter, may be divided into ten parts, and each part gets the prefix "deci" (decimeter), the same prefix used in the word *decimal,* which describes a number used in the scale of tens. The decimeter may be split into ten equal parts, each with the prefix "centi." The centimeter is the one-hundredth part of a meter. Similarly, in United States coinage a cent is one-hundredth part of a dollar.

A thousand base units are indicated by the prefix "kilo." And Americans are familiar with kilowatts, meaning one thousand watts, and kilocycles, the term for one thousand cycles used in radio broadcasting frequencies.

A complete set of these prefixes may be applied to any metric unit. In decimal intervals measurements of length range from a billion meters (a gigameter) to one billionth of a meter (a nanometer), and even extend to trillions and beyond. (For other multiples, see the table, "Prefixes for Metric Units," on page 118.)

However, for common usage only a small number of terms need be memorized—plus the simple fact that the metric scales go up and down in powers of ten.

Because it eliminates complicated methods of calculating, a decimal measuring system offers fewer chances of error. Metric measurement is a way of saving time and avoiding trouble.

Chaos or Coherence?

At a meeting recently where business and government leaders talked about the metric system, one businessman thundered on for more than an hour about "the great and glorious traditional American system of weights and measures."

"Will the speaker answer some questions?" a member of the audience politely asked. When the speaker agreed, he was given these four queries:

How many acres in a square mile?

How many cubic inches in a bushel?

How long is each side of a square one-acre lot?

What is the weight of a quart of water?

The speaker was left speechless. His questioner went on to point out that in American schools the customary tables of measurement are among the most difficult studies for the pupil to master. Hard to memorize, they are also easy to forget.

In any metric country, however, the schoolchild can readily answer questions on units of length and area, and on how a volume of water in cubic meters is related to its mass in kilograms.

The United States Table of Weights and Measures in common usage contains two kinds of miles, 56 kinds of bushels, eight kinds of tons, two kinds of pounds, three kinds of ounces.

Today's farmer, who operates a tractor, still measures his land by the acre—defined as an area that could once be plowed in a day with a yoke of oxen. He reckons his corn crop in bushels, which have no clear link to any other units of measurement. The bushels need to be translated into tons for purposes of shipping. But when the corn is stored, it is not measured either in bushels or tons. Storage space is calculated in cubic feet! There is no simple relationship between any of these measurements.

If a surveyor laid out a field that was perfectly square and one acre in size, he could not make it come out in even numbers. Each side would have to be 208 feet, 8 inches long! Not many years ago the surveyor of the property also had to be sure he was using the correct foot. Surveyors in Brooklyn, New York, recognized four different feet as legal

—the United States foot, the Bushwick foot, the Williams-burg foot, and the foot of the 26th Ward!

The American carpenter buys so-called one-inch lumber in widths of 2 inches, 3 inches, 4 inches, and so on. But the craftsman finds that his "one-inch" lumber actually measures ¾ inches if seasoned, and $25/32$ inches if green, or unseasoned. In width a "four-inch" board is either $3\frac{1}{2}$ inches or $3\frac{9}{16}$ inches. Little wonder that the carpenter spends more time figuring and less time building. He is forced to calculate in what are called vulgar fractions if he is to be precise in his work.

The metric system does away with the problems of dividing sixteenths by fifths or adding $3\frac{2}{3}$ to $9\frac{5}{64}$. Metric calculation is decimal throughout, centered around the use of the decimal point. With the fast growing use of computers, slide rules and calculating machines, vulgar fractions are becoming more and more obsolete in the business, science, and engineering worlds.

The metric system has eliminated the need for a separate series for dry measures and for liquid measures. Volume and capacity are both expressed in the same metric units.

Milk and gasoline are bought by the liter in metric countries. Here is an example of how carefully the planners of the metric system went about linking together the units of length, volume, and mass: the liter is a cube that in width, breadth, and height is exactly one decimeter, a tenth of a meter.

To unify metric units even further, the liter was planned not only as a measure of volume or capacity, but also as a measure of mass or what is loosely called weight. A one-liter container was designed to hold a quantity of pure water at a specific temperature with a mass of one kilogram. This link between size and mass is still a useful one—even though it is no longer precise enough for scientific purposes.

The metric system not only unified measurements of all kinds with simple decimal ratios, it also corrected a false idea about weight that has been outmoded since the days of Isaac Newton.

Weight and Mass

In today's England Isaac Newton's mass would be measured in kilograms. His weight could be measured in newtons.

If that seems confusing, it is because the inch-pound nations of the world, including the United States, have never fully embodied Newton's discoveries into their measuring system.

Three centuries ago Isaac Newton pointed out that in everyday life the term "weight" is used for what is really mass. "I call mass the quantity of matter," said Newton.

However, weight is a force—the force exerted by gravitational pull. The force of gravity exerted on an object by the earth decreases with its distance from the earth's center. When an astronaut is in orbit a hundred miles above the earth, his weight has changed even though his mass remains the same.

Despite Newton's discoveries the "English" system continued to use the same unit for both weight and mass—the pound. Scientists and engineers adopted units which they used in their technical work to distinguish weight as a force from mass as a quantity of matter. In everyday use the old system of measurement lumped together weight and mass, even though it was clear that a gold bar did not weigh the same in a laboratory in the mountains of Geneva, Switzerland, as it did at the Royal Observatory in Greenwich, England, near sea level.

The confusion about the terms "weight" and "mass" left people ill-prepared to understand how space travel affects weight. In recent years television viewers around the world have seen that an astronaut on the surface of the moon weighs much less than on earth, making them aware that weight varies with the force of gravity. Nevertheless, even in the metric nations, people still speak of weight in terms of mass units to signify the quantity of matter.

In the metric system weight as a force is measured in terms of the metric unit of force, called the newton. A force of 1 newton, when applied for 1 second, will give to a 1-kilogram mass a speed of 1 meter per second. The newton is the metric unit for measuring not only the force of gravity but any other force as well.

The metric unit of mass is the kilogram. This is the only base unit that has not been defined in terms of a phenomenon of nature. The standard for the kilogram is a highly polished cylinder of platinum-iridium alloy which is maintained in a vault in Sèvres, with a replica kept at the National Bureau of Standards.

From a few basic units which are the building blocks of metric measurement, the Système International d'Unités (SI) has put together a series of so-called derived units. These combine the scales of units of length, mass, and time, to form additional measuring units.

The joule is the unit for energy or work. Power is measured in watts. The volt denotes electric potential. Pressure is indicated in terms of the unit called the pascal.

The ampere measures the magnitude of electric current. This is considered a basic SI unit, along with the candela, for luminous intensity. The mole is used for the molecular quantity of substance which may be determined through chemical analysis.

New SI units are devised as they are needed by the sciences probing new areas of research. However, the metric system has drawn on the past for its basic units of temperature and time.

One Hundred Degrees

Few people have need for a thermometer that can measure the extreme cold of outer space or the intense heat on the planet Venus. The metric thermometer, using what is known as the Kelvin scale, can record such unearthly ranges of temperature.

At the same time that it serves science the metric system also answers the practical needs of those who are still earthbound. The Celsius thermometer can be used for forecasting the weather, testing the bath water, signifying when a roast is done. This scale became part of the metric system in 1927.

Anders Celsius, a Swedish astronomer who lived in the early eighteenth century, did not invent the first thermometer. Both Galileo and Newton long before him had experimented with glass-tube instruments for measuring temperature. But in 1742 Celsius devised a mercury thermometer with a range of 100 degrees. He designated 0 degrees as the temperature of melting ice and 100 degrees as that of boiling water. He then calibrated the degrees between the two extremes.

Celsius's thermometer, also called the centigrade thermometer, became one of several temperature-measuring instruments that were in use through the nineteenth century.

In 1714 the German physicist Gabriel Daniel Fahrenheit
had devised his thermometer with its zero at the freezing
point of salt water. The Fahrenheit scale rose by a series of
12-degree steps to 96 degrees, which he believed to be the
temperature of his own body. In later research it was determined that nature did not quite accord with Fahrenheit's
scale of twelves. The normal human body temperature is
actually 98.6 degrees. Nor did boiling water at 212 degrees
Fahrenheit fit neatly into the intended scheme of twelves.
However, this type of thermometer came into wide use and
was accepted in the United States.

A British scientist, Lord Kelvin, extended the decimal-
based thermometer, taking as his zero point the so-called
absolute zero—273.16 degrees below the zero point on the
Celsius scale. In 1948 the Kelvin scale was adopted into the
metric system, along with the Celsius scale. The Kelvin
scale is used almost exclusively by scientists.

The common thread running through the metric units is
the decimal ratio of tens—with two exceptions. For measuring time and angles the modern metric system held to
the method of the ancients.

Unit of Time

Over the centuries, man con-
tinued to search for a standard in nature with which to
measure length. But he has long had such a natural guide
for measuring time.

Four thousand years ago astronomers in Mesopotamia

viewed the heavens as a clock that marked out the years and ticked off the seconds. The sun, the moon, the stars, the earth became mankind's timekeepers. And when the metric system came along its inventors needed only to include a unit of time that was already known and accepted world-wide.

The second is the official SI basic unit of time. Here the metric system breaks away from its pattern of tens. From olden days has come a method of reckoning time in cycles of 6 and 60, and of 6 times 60, or 360.

Early Sumerian astronomers, who believed that there were 360 days in the year, divided the day into 360 equal parts. The base figure of 60 was later applied to the path of the sun in the heavens and to the whole circle of the horizon. From these early studies came not only the accepted standards of time but also the division of our circle into 360 parts, or degrees.

When adopted as the metric unit of time, the second was defined in terms of the rotation of the earth as it makes its way around the sun. But the earth is no longer considered an accurate timekeeper. Now, precisely redefined in scientific terms, the second remains the universal unit of time.

Scientists at the international metric bureau have found a highly accurate method of fixing the duration of one second—more precise than the tick of the finest clock. They take as their standard the radiation activity of one form of a metal called cesium—the isotope cesium-133. The metric second is now equivalent to the duration of 9,192,631,770 cycles of the radiation emitted by cesium-133 under specific conditions. It may be a long time before scientists need a more clearly defined second than that!

The combination of the metric unit of time with the

unit of length or distance has produced the SI unit for
speed, the meter per second. For the motorist the more familiar speed unit is the kilometer per hour. If the United
States changes to metric usage, a driver on the highway will
no longer watch his speedometer to see whether he is
"going 50." The rough equivalent to 50 miles per hour
would be 80 kilometers per hour.

For a great many people America's going metric is not an
"if" but a "when." They see the likelihood that the changeover may come as this country celebrates an important
anniversary.

In 1776 this nation came into existence, already wonder-
ing how to get rid of its cumbersome system of weights and
measures. By 1876 the United States entered its second century as one of the nations signing the Treaty of the Meter,
pledged to support the international metric system. Will
the United States begin its third century in 1976 as a metric
nation?

CHANGE

IS

STRANGE

Few people realized how swiftly America could become accustomed to dial telephones. Or to automobile seat belts. Or to zip codes.

Rapid change is a familiar feature of American life. Outworn ideas, attitudes, customs, institutions seem to disappear quickly—once people are convinced that something better is at hand.

However, this country has taken its time in making up its mind about the advantages of the metric system. Almost two centuries have passed since Jefferson foresaw "a future time when the citizens of the United States may be induced to undertake a thorough reformation of their whole system of measures. . . ."

John Quincy Adams noted that "opinion is the queen of the world," and that the America of his day was not yet ready to adopt the metric system, which he considered superior to any other.

Opinion has changed. The swing toward the metric system is already being made by a large part of the United States. Repeatedly, polls of public opinion taken on the streets of American towns reveal a steady trend toward metric usage and approval. The polls also show that the more people get to know about the metric system, the more they favor its complete adoption.

The decision for this nation to go metric could not be made by any small group of officials in Washington. It could come only when the great majority of the people were convinced that the metric system was good for America.

Metric advocates do not intend to force new measuring units on the public. However, a number of efforts are being made to encourage wider metric usage, to help carry out a voluntary plan that will lead to an orderly changeover.

A majority of American businessmen, soberly facing the immense cost of going metric, have approved the change. They regard it as an investment which will eventually be profitable in terms of saving time, effort, and money, as well as improving the sale of American goods in what has now become a metric world market.

For the first time in this century, the United States by the 1970s had lost its so-called favorable balance-of-trade.

Suddenly this nation was importing more goods than it exported to foreign countries. There were many reasons for the United States loss of trade. But one of them was the fact that this country was offering its inch-pound products to a meter-kilogram world.

Since the cost of doing business with metric countries increased each year, there was no longer sense in putting off the change as long as possible. American corporations began to realize the price of remaining on the "English" system. "In effect," said one United States official, "we are trying to sell left-handed tools to people who are right-handed."

Some American firms moved their plants to foreign lands. Others were buying manufactured metric parts abroad, adapting them to inch-pound production methods, and then trying to sell the finished goods to metric countries. This nation was being hindered by the burden of using two measuring systems at the same time. Each year the United States was paying increasingly heavy penalty for being out of step with the rest of the world.

Business leaders realized that the cost of a change to metric would be a large but one-time expense—while the benefits would go on endlessly. Some inch-pound machinery would need to be scrapped. Much of it could be converted. Most machines wear out in a few years and they could then be replaced with metric machines.

Business and labor leaders also looked carefully at the problem of retraining workers. Here they were encouraged by the example of other countries where the retraining process was much easier than had been expected. For the average American family the changeover would be little different from that successfully achieved by the British, Chinese, or Nigerian family.

The challenge to the American people has been a difficult one. But this country had met crises before with courage, common sense, and high spirits.

The electronic computer could be America's bridge to the metric system. The huge calculating problems posed by metric changeover could readily be fed into the computers, which figure at lightning speed. For example, a study at one Cleveland steel warehouse estimated that its entire inventory list of steel sheets and strips, bars and coils could be converted to metric sizes in a few hours.

Television was seen as the other important means for the switch to metric. The main information about the meter, the liter, the kilogram could be brought by television into millions of American homes. Through programs prepared with imagination and wit people of all ages could quickly learn the simple essentials of the new units and how to use them.

America might have changed to metric a hundred years ago. But perhaps there never was, or will be, a better time than now.

Horse and Buggy

America is a motor-minded nation, geared to the speed and power of automobile, jet plane, and spaceship. How strange it is that today's power sources are still being measured in horse and buggy terms!

Two hundred years ago James Watt hitched a work horse to a load and estimated the number of pounds that the animal could pull over a given vertical distance. Watt was trying to use the horse's effort to measure the amount of work performed by his steam engine. That was how Watt invented the measuring unit, the horsepower.

In the United States the motor is still rated in horsepower. But this work horse of an old measuring system is being put out to pasture. Power of any kind is now measured in metric terms by the watt, named for the man who developed the steam engine that replaced the work horse.

Because basic metric units are defined by the most advanced scientific methods there is no longer any uncertainty as to what they stand for. The metric system is open-ended, meaning that it is designed for constant improvement. Since the system was invented the standards have gradually been made more precise. Also, new units are added as needed. One advantage for the United States in going metric is that this country will be able to play a more active part in developing new units and standards.

For example, metrologists of the world are at work on a project aiming to limit the growing noise pollution which is afflicting this planet. The first task in achieving that result is to find a suitable unit for the measurement of sound.

Every nation adopting the metric system went through a useful period of clearing out the obsolete leftovers of outmoded measuring standards. For one thing the changeover swept away many old container sizes that had long since failed to serve any practical purpose. American storekeepers and shoppers are often confused by the array of odd-sized jars and bottles, cans and packages that have long cluttered up the grocery shelves. These could be reduced to a few standardized metric sizes.

Metal fasteners, nuts, and bolts may also be due for a weeding out of unnecessary varieties. The same may be true of plumbing pipes and fittings, lumber, building hardware, bricks, tile, as well as many kinds of tools. Simplifying sizes will in turn reduce the paper work, record keeping, and space needed for storage and warehousing.

The United States has been gradually using more and more metric measurement. Should that random trend be allowed to continue in its haphazard fashion, or would it be wiser to change by plan?

The rate of drift toward metric usage is so slow that decades would pass while America was still struggling with two systems of measurement, suffering costly production and trade losses.

Every nation changing to a new way of measuring has had to carry out the plan at its own pace. Japan had serious problems in its slow off-and-on progress toward metric adoption over a period of forty years. Other countries that planned on a rapid change found they had to readjust their goals to a slower pace. Most nations found that ten years was a suitable span of time in which an orderly change can be made.

Unlike Great Britain and Australia, the United States does not have the double problem of converting its coinage while also revising its measurements. Another advantage for the United States is that this is the last inch-pound country, and here the old system can be completely abandoned forever since it will not be in use anywhere else in the world. Once America completes its changeover, there will no longer be any need for conversion tables. The people of the United States can go metric through "learn-by-using" methods rather than by memorizing the metric and inch-pound equivalents.

This country can profit by the experience of all other countries. Some have found the change to metric more difficult than others. In some nations the planning was vague and uncharted. Others detailed the changeover steps for each section of the population. The shift in many cases began with those business firms engaged with raw materi-

als, heavy industry, and wholesale operations, gradually including those dealing in finished products, light manufacturing, and retail trade.

In smoothing the path to metric changeover, British
planners put much emphasis on metric education in the
schools. British children have learned quickly. In turn they
have become teachers of metric usage in their homes and
communities.

Learn by Doing

THINK METRIC!

A banner above the blackboard spells out the message.
This is a Detroit suburban classroom. Its pupils are well advanced into the metric world.

In the center of the floor is a taped area which is 1 square
meter in size. A dictionary on a stand bears the label, "This
book weighs 1 kilogram." An aquarium is filled with exactly 10 liters of water. "The water in this tank has a mass
of 10 kilograms," states a small sign. Each day begins with
the class's checking the room temperature on the Celsius
thermometer.

The children play a simple game. The teacher holds up a
1-meter stick. Each pupil looks at the stick and tries to
chalk off on the blackboard a distance of 1 meter, 2 meters,
3 meters. These estimates are measured to see who came
closest.

"If I cut this stick into 10 parts," asks the teacher, each
part would be what?"

"A decimeter."

"Or cut it into 100 parts?"

"A centimeter."

Eventually, in a metric America, learning the metric system will be as easy as it is to learn French in France. Many school systems in the United States and far-seeing schoolteachers are not waiting for the complete transition. They are giving their pupils a head start in metric education.

The most simple and direct style of teaching proves to be the best. A classroom might be asked to memorize tables of metric units and complex lists of conversions from "English" to metric. But far better results are achieved with the use of simple metric tools, enabling the students to learn by measuring—to think in metric terms. On metric balances they can weigh out a quantity of sand or water. Meter sticks and tapes are available and can even be made by the pupils. The one-liter measuring cup, calibrated in cubic centimeters, can become a familiar classroom tool.

Measuring tasks become an absorbing game as the students discover the metric measurements of the teacher's desk, the area of the room, the dimensions of a guinea pig, the mass of an orange, one another's height, and the measurements of their books. For example, the width of the full lines of type in this book is 10.64 centimeters, and the length of this page is 23.50 centimeters and its width is 15.56 centimeters.

Nor is metric learning limited to the arithmetic class. Geography is a subject in which the student can test his metric skills. A challenging field is map reading, with distances on maps shown in kilometers and elevation in meters.

Undoubtedly the schools will offer new textbooks as well as new teaching aids for learning the metric system. A simple educational device is a set of ten plastic tiles. Each tile is 1 decimeter (or 10 centimeters) square, and 1 centimeter thick. The ten tiles fit neatly into a clear plastic container which is 1 cubic decimeter in capacity. The empty cube may also be filled to the top with exactly 1 liter of water. The water has a mass of 1 kilogram.

Although the complete language of metric measurement covers every technical and scientific need, it is not necessary to know more than a few metric terms for ordinary use. The abbreviations for each metric unit, such as "m" for meter and "kg" for kilogram, must be memorized, along with the main prefixes for the multiples of the units in powers of ten.

The abbreviated way of writing "square meter" is m². A cubic meter is denoted by m³. A useful unit for measuring land is the hectare, which is 10,000 square meters and is quaintly abbreviated as "ha."

A new method is now preferred thoughout the metric world in the writing of large numbers, such as thousands, millions, and billions. A space is used, instead of the traditional comma, to separate each successive group of three places to the left and to the right of the decimal point. For example, a meter is shown as equal to 1 650 763.73 wavelengths of orange-red radiation emitted by krypton-86.

Decimal usage means that less time is spent in the classroom on vulgar fractions and the problems of finding the least common denominator. The metric system is expected to put an end to old-fashioned methods of calculating that have been a painful study for many generations of both teachers and pupils.

Moving the decimal point is the simple way up and down any scale of metric units. In units of length, for example, 3085 centimeters may be written as 30.85 meters or as .03085 kilometers.

Research has shown that using the metric system could

save up to 25 per cent of the time spent in teaching arithmetic. Multiply that by the fifty million students in American schools to get some idea of the time wasted in learning a nonmetric system.

World-wide metric unity becomes an important tool which serves each nation and all mankind. The common speech of the metric system is soon to be spoken everywhere—in the stadium where athletes compete for medals, in the international meetings where men gather to solve the world's problems, in the market places around the globe.

Metric language is used in exploring outer space. Universal measurement in metric terms may yet make the difference between life and death for explorers imperiled in the silent reaches beyond the earth.

A Measure of Harmony

Lost in space! The very idea chills the heart. And yet this is the risk that men face as they begin to venture into environments beyond the earth.

What happens to a party of astronauts whose disabled capsule drifts out of control through outer space? A rescue mission will soon be possible. An agreement between the United States and the Soviet Union provides for international rendezvous and docking. The plan calls for the adapting of equipment so that spacecraft from both nations can become joined in space. The methods and hardware are to be perfectly matched in metric measurements.

In a universal metric world many things become possible, or at least easier to accomplish. With billions to feed the metric nations now find it simpler to measure the global wheat crop against the need. Using common units of measurement, all the countries stand a better chance of dealing with damage to the natural environment. With airlines circling the globe each day, the giant jets will be easier to service when they are built to metric specifications and when metric-sized tools, equipment, and spare parts are available at every international airport.

Men and women of science agreed long ago to use metric units. The same terms are used throughout the world in discussing the measurement of distant stars, in probing ocean depths, in monitoring the weather conditions of the world. An entire continent, Antarctica, is being measured in metric terms by scientists from many nations. Those at work in the field of public health now have a universal language for interchanging information on disease, medical procedures, equipment, and medicines.

In a quiet suburb of Paris, where the Seine runs along a grassy bank, stands the international palace of the meter. On a huge map inside the impressive building the countries of the world are colored green as one by one they adopt metric usage. Gradually, almost the entire world has turned green.

The map tells an inspiring story of global unity. Even countries that for centuries could agree on very little, are now united on the meter. The metric countries include both the capitalist and the socialist states as well as the so-called third-world nations which are not committed to either economic system.

On the metric map are represented the heavily industrialized countries and also those that have little industry. The giants among nations are there as well as the little ones, the newest, and the oldest. The homelands of Galileo,

Kepler, and Newton are metric, as is the entire modern scientific world which they helped bring into being.

For the past two hundred years a bitter controversy has raged over the system called metric. The conflict is now all but ended.

There are some things left in the world for nations to fight about. But measurement is no longer one of them.

TABLES

Prefixes for Metric Units

Metric Multiples		Powers	Prefixes	Pronunciations	Abbreviations
1 000 000 000 000	=	10^{12}	tera	ter'a	T
1 000 000 000	=	10^9	giga	ji'ga	G
1 000 000	=	10^6	mega	meg'a	M
1 000	=	10^3	kilo	kil'o	k
100	=	10^2	hecto	hek'to	h
10	=	10^1	deka	dek'a	da
1	=	10^0			
0.1	=	10^{-1}	deci	des'i	d
0.01	=	10^{-2}	centi	sen'ti	c
0.001	=	10^{-3}	milli	mil'i	m
0.000 001	=	10^{-6}	micro	mi'kro	μ
0.000 000 001	=	10^{-9}	nano	nan'o	n
0.000 000 000 001	=	10^{-12}	pico	pe'ko	p
0.000 000 000 000 001	=	10^{-15}	femto	fem'to	f
0.000 000 000 000 000 001	=	10^{-18}	atto	at'to	a

Definitions of Basic Metric Units

Length METER (m)

The meter is defined as 1 650 763.73 wavelengths in vacuum of the orange-red line of the spectrum of krypton-86.

Time SECOND (s)

The second is defined as the duration of 9 192 631 770 cycles of the radiation associated with a specified transition of the cesium-133 atom. It is realized by tuning an oscillator to the resonance frequency of the cesium atoms as they pass through a system of magnets and a resonant cavity into a detector.

Mass KILOGRAM (kg)

The standard for the unit of mass, the kilogram, is a cylinder of platinum-iridium alloy kept by the International Bureau of Weights and Measures in France. A duplicate in the custody of the National Bureau of Standards serves as the mass standard for the United States.

Temperature
KELVIN (K)

The thermodynamic or Kelvin scale of temperature has its zero point at absolute zero and the triple point of water (the temperature at which water exists in all three states—vapor, liquid, and solid) is defined as 273.16 kelvins. The Celsius scale is derived from the Kelvin scale. The triple point on the Celsius scale is defined as 0.01° C, which is approximately 32.02° F. on the Fahrenheit scale.

Electric Current
AMPERE (A)

The ampere is defined as the magnitude of the current that, when flowing through each of two long parallel wires separated by one meter in free space, results in a force between the two wires (caused by their magnetic fields) of 2 $\times 10^{-7}$ newtons for each meter of length.

Luminous Intensity
CANDELA (cd)

The candela is defined as the luminous intensity of $\frac{1}{600\,000}$ of a square meter of the cone of light emitted by a blackbody cavity heated to a temperature of 2042K, the melting point of platinum.

Common Conversion Factors

	Given the number of	To obtain the number of	Multiply by the factor of
LENGTH	inches	centimeters (cm)	2.54
	feet	decimeters (dm)	3.05
	yards	meters (m)	0.91
	miles	kilometers (km)	1.61
	millimeters (mm)	inches	0.039
	centimeters	inches	0.39
	meters	yards	1.09
	kilometers	miles	0.62

	Given the number of	To obtain the number of	Multiply by the factor of
AREA	square inches	square centimeters (cm²)	6.45
	square feet	square meters (m²)	0.093
	square yards	square meters	0.84
	square miles	square kilometers (km²)	2.59
	acres	hectares (ha)	0.40
	square centimeters	square inches	0.16
	square meters	square yards	1.20
	square kilometers	square miles	0.39
	hectares	acres	2.47
MASS OR WEIGHT	grains	milligrams (mg)	64.8
	ounces	grams (g)	28.3
	pounds	kilograms (kg)	0.45
	short tons	megagrams (metric tons)	0.91
	milligrams	grains	0.015
	grams	ounces	0.035
	kilograms	pounds	2.21
	megagrams	short tons	1.10
CAPACITY OR VOLUME	fluid ounces	milliliter (ml)	29.8
	pints (fluid)	liters (l)	0.47
	quarts (fluid)	liters	0.95
	gallons (fluid)	liters	3.80
	cubic inches	cubic centimeters (cm³)	16.4
	cubic feet	cubic meters (m³)	0.028
	cubic feet	liters	28.3
	bushels (dry)	liters	35.2
	milliliters	ounces	0.034
	liters	pints	2.11
	liters	quarts	1.06
	liters	gallons	0.26
	liters	cubic feet	0.035
	cubic centimeters	cubic inches	0.061
	cubic meters	cubic feet	35.3
	cubic meters	bushels	28.4
VELOCITY	feet per second	meters per second	0.305
	miles per hour	kilometers per hour	1.609
	meters per second	feet per second	3.281
	kilometers per hour	miles per hour	0.621
TEMPERATURE	degrees Fahrenheit	degrees Celsius	0.556 (after subtracting 32)
	degrees Celsius	degrees Fahrenheit	1.80 (then add 32)

SUGGESTIONS
FOR FURTHER
READING

ASIMOV, ISAAC. *Realm of Measure*. Houghton Mifflin, 1960. Although somewhat dated, this book contains a lively account of the history of weights and measures, written by a well-known scientist and science writer.

DE SIMONE, DANIEL V. *A Metric America*. National Bureau of Standards Special Publication 345, 1971. This easy-to-read report summarizes the three-year United States Metric Study and was written by its director. The subtitle is "A Decision Whose Time Has Come."

DONOVAN, FRANK. *Prepare Now for a Metric Future*. Weybright and Talley, 1970. A skillful writer recounts the background of the metric system and deals with the practical problems of applying it to the needs of the United States today.

PAGE, CHESTER H., AND VIGOUREAUX, PAUL, EDITORS. *The International System of Units (SI)*. National Bureau of Standards Special Publication 330, 1971. In concise form, this booklet contains the official units and standards of the metric system, including the most recent revisions made by the General Conference of Weights and Measures.

INDEX

Abbreviations, for metric units, 114
Absolute zero, 103
Acre, land measured by, 98
Adams, John Quincy, 53, 54, 56, 57, 58, 107
Africa, metric system adopted by, 91
Air pollution, 11
American Revolution, 25, 34
Ampere, 102
Antarctica, 90, 116
Apothecaries' weight, 30
Armstretch (fathom), 15
Around the World in Eighty Days (Verne), 70
Asia, metric system adopted by, 91
Assizes, 62
Astronomy, 55; measurements in, 21, 104
Australia, metric system adopted by, 92
Automation, 89
Avoirdupois, 30

Bell, Alexander Graham, 84, 85, 86
Body, human, as measuring stick, 14–17, 26
Burke, Thomas, 73
Bushel, 29, 61, 62, 81, 98

Caesar, Julius, 36
Calendar, republican, in France, 47–48
Canada, metric system adopted by, 92
Candela, 102
Carat, 30
Celsius, Anders, 102
Celsius (centigrade) scale, 95, 102, 103
Centimeter, 97, 112, 113
Ceres (ship), 25, 30
Cesium-133, and metric second, 104
Chain, surveyor's, 30
Chemistry, 55; transformed by Lavoisier, 32, 34
China, metric system adopted by, 88
Civil War, 65
Coast and Geodetic Survey, U.S., 50, 52

Coinage, in early U.S., 26, 27, 28
Colombia, metric system adopted by, 64
Commerce Department, U.S., 92
Computer, electronic, 89, 109
Connecticut, metric system taught in schools of, 64
Cord, woodcutter's, 30
Cubit, 15, 16

Dalmatia, 52
Decimal inch, 89
Decimal system, 26, 27, 28, 96
Decimeter, 96, 97, 112, 113, 114
Declaration of Independence, 32
Dickens, Charles, 60, 61
Dollar, as standard of U.S. money, 27
Dombey, Citizen, 42–43
Double pace, 16, 36
Dram, fluid, 30
Dubrovnik (Dalmatia), and statue of Roland, 52

Early, Jubal, 65
Earth, measurement of, 40–41
Earth sciences, 50
Electric inductance, Henry's research in, 68
Electric units of measure, 101–102
Electronic computer, 89, 109
Elizabeth I, 62
England, 24, 30, 48, 55, 57, 58; assizes in, 62; debates in, on changing weights and measures, 42, 73–74; and fire in Houses of Parliament (1834), 60, 61, 62; Jefferson's visit to, 34–35; metric system adopted by, 92; standards of measurement in, destroyed by fire (1834), 61; and tallies in vaults of Parliament, 61
English Channel, 71
Enlightenment, 23, 31–32, 34
Exchange Service, global, for use of scientists, 67

Fahrenheit, Gabriel Daniel, 103
Fahrenheit scale, 103
Fathom, 15, 16

Finger widths, as standards for units of length, 15, 16

Foot, 15, 17, 36, 37, 39, 40, 43, 44, 96; different kinds of, 98–99

Ford Motor Co., metric measurements used by, 95

Fractions, vulgar, 99, 114

France, 24, 30, 42, 48, 53, 55, 57, 58, 63, 69, 70, 74; earth-measuring project in, 40–41; Jefferson's visit to, 31, 32, 33, 34; metric map in, 116; metric system adopted by, 63; Michelson's visit to, 77, 78; republican calendar in, 47–48

French Revolution, 25, 40

Furlong, 30, 96

Galileo, 19, 20, 21, 24, 39, 76, 90, 102, 116

Gallon, 29, 61

Gauge, railroad, 81

Geography, and metric system, 113

George III, 34

Germany, metric system adopted by, 63

Gigameter, 97

Grain, as unit of weight, 30

Gram, 33

Gravity, 100, 101; newton as metric unit for measuring, 101; and Newton's formula, 22–23; pendulum as device for measuring force of, 20, 40

Greece, ancient, 57

Greenwich, Royal Observatory in, 101

Guillotin, Joseph Ignace, 32

Guinea, metric system adopted by, 91

Handspan, 15, 16

Hassler, Ferdinand Rudolph, 49–50, 51–52, 94

Heavens, charting of, 21, 104

Hectare, 114

Henry, Joseph, 65, 66, 67, 68

Henry, as unit of inductance, 68

Hogshead, 29

Horsepower, 109, 110

Human body, as measuring stick, 14–17, 26

Hundredweight, 30

Huntsville (Ala.), metric measurements used in, 95

IGY (International Geophysical Year), 90, 91

Inch, 37, 96; decimal, 89

Industrial Revolution: American, 55; English, 35

Interferometer, 77

International Bureau of Weights and Measures, 70

International Geophysical Year (IGY), 90, 91

International Institute for Preserving and Perfecting Anglo-Saxon Weights and Measures, 72

Isolationism, in U.S., 88

Japan, 111; metric system adopted by, 91, 92

Jefferson, 24–45 passim, 107; in England, 34–35; in France, 31, 32, 33, 34; Hassler hired by, 50; and Lavoisier, 32, 33, 34, 42; in New York City, 38, 39; and pendulum plan for new unit of length, 39–40, 43–44; as President, 45; as Secretary of State, 38, 39, 42, 44; U.S. money system devised by, 27, 28; and U.S. weights and measures, new plan for, 38, 39, 43–46

Johnson, Andrew, 66

Joule, 101

Kelvin, Lord, 103

Kelvin scale, 102, 103

Kepler, Johannes, 21, 22, 24, 90, 117

Kilocycle, 97

Kilogram, 65, 74, 99, 101, 114

Kilometer, 105

Kilowatt, 81, 97

Knot, as unit of ship's speed, 30

Krypton-86, as wavelength basis for metric standard, 13, 78, 114

Latin, as language of the learned, 24

Latin America, metric system adopted by, 74

Latitude, 22

Lavoisier, Antoine, 32, 33, 34, 41, 42

League, as measure of distance, 29

Length, unit of, in measurement systems, 13, 14

Libra (pound), 36

Light: nature of, 77; speed of, measured by Michelson, 76

Liter, 99, 113, 114

Long ton, 30, 85

Longitude, 35

Lumber, measurement of, 99

Lydia, coinage in, 35

Mail, international, metric system used in, 67

Map reading, and metric system, 113

Mass, and weight, 100–101

Mass production, 56

Mesopotamia, astronomers of, 104

Meter, 12, 13, 46, 47, 48, 65, 76, 96; defined in terms of wavelength of light from krypton-86, 13, 78, 114; and measurement of meridian, 41, 47; metal bar as model of, 47; per second, 105

Metes and bounds, 45

Metric map, in Paris, 116

Metric Study, U.S., 93

Metric system, 47, 48, 51, 52, 53, 55, 62, 69, 70, 96; abbreviations used in, 114; and Adams, 53, 54, 56, 57, 58, 107; advantages of, 10–11, 54, 113–16; and Bell, 84, 85, 86; capacity measured in, 99; completeness of, 13; and computer, 109; in Connecticut schools, 64; decimal calculations throughout, 96–97, 99, 114; force measured in, 101; and global unity, 116–17; and Hassler, 51, 52, 94; and Henry, 66, 68, 94; holdouts against, 92; learning, in U.S. schools, 112–13; as legal source of reference for official U.S. measurements, 74, 95; legalized in U.S. (1866), 66–67; and mail, international, 67; mass measured in, 101; and Michelson, 76, 77, 78; and Napoleon

Bonaparte, 52, 53; in Olympic Games, 73, 95; as open-ended system, 110; opposition to, in U.S. (1920s), 87–89; power measured in, 101, 110; pros and cons of, argued in U.S. (1870s), 71–73; and recommendations of U.S. Metric Study (1971), 93; in science, universal use of, 76, 116, 117; simplicity of, 13; and Stratton, 82, 83, 86; teaching, in U.S. schools, 112–13; television in U.S. as means of conveying information about, 109; temperature measured in, 102–103; time measured in, 103–105; trend toward, in U.S., 107, 111; in U.S. factories (1820s), 56; volume measured in, 99; weight measured in, 101; and world unity, 116–17

Metrology, 64, 70, 74, 75, 76, 77, 110

Michelson, Albert A., 75, 76, 77, 78, 79, 80, 94; in France, 77, 78; speed of light measured by, 76; work of, in metrology, 77–78

Mile, 16, 36, 96; as confusing measure, 36; nautical, 36

Milligram, 95

Minim, 30

Mole (gram molecule), 102

Money system, Jefferson's plan for, 27, 28

Musket factory, Whitney's, 56

Nanometer, 97

Napoleon Bonaparte, 46, 52, 55; and metric system, 52, 53

NASA (National Aeronautics and Space Administration), 95, 96

National Academy of Sciences, 65

National Aeronautics and Space Administration (NASA), 95, 96

National Bureau of Standards, 80, 81, 83, 92, 101

Nautical mile, 36

Navigation, 23

New England, 64

New York City, Jefferson in, 38, 39

New York Times, 82

New Zealand, metric system adopted by, 92

Newton, Isaac, 22, 23, 24, 35, 39, 100, 102, 117

Newton, as unit of force, 100, 101

Noise pollution, 110

Odometer, 45–46

Office of Weights and Measures, U.S., and International Prototype Meter and Kilogram, 74

Olympic Games, metric system used in, 73, 95

Ounce: fluid, 30; as unit of weight, 30

Pace, double, 16, 36

Pacing, field measured by, 14–15

Pascal, as unit of pressure, 102

Peck, 29

Pedometer, 31

Pendulum, 19, 20, 39, 40, 42, 43; as device for measuring time, 20; and Jefferson's plan for new unit of length, 39–40, 43–44

Pennyweight, 29, 30

Physics, 55

Pica, 30

Pied-de-roi, 41

Pinch, as measure, 15

Pint, 29, 30

Planetary motions, Kepler's laws of, 21, 22

Platinum-iridium cylinder, as standard for kilogram, 101

Platinum-uranium bar in Washington, and meter standard in France, 75

Pound: as unit of money, 35; as unit of weight, 17, 30, 35, 61, 65

Printing, invention of, 17

Quality control, in factories, 89

Quart, 29

Report to Congress on Weights and Measures (Adams), 54, 57

Rod, as unit of length, 15, 96

Roland, statue of, in Dubrovnik, 52

Rome, ancient, 16, 36, 37, 57

Science: becomes international, 24; metric system used in, 76, 116, 117; and new electrical age, 68; precise measurements in, 18, 20, 24, 29, 64, 74

Scruple, as unit of weight, 30

Second, as official SI unit of time, 104

Sèvres (France), metric palace in, 69, 70, 74–75, 101

Shaku-kan, 91

SI (Système International d'Unités), 101, 102, 104, 105

Silliman's Journal, 55

Smithsonian Institution, 65, 66, 67, 68

Soviet Union: and agreement with U.S. on space operations, 115; metric system adopted by, 88

Space Age, 90

Span, as unit of length, 15, 16

Sputnik, 90

Stans, Maurice H., 93

Stockholm Conference on Human Environment (1972), 11

Stratton, Samuel W., 79, 80, 81, 82, 83, 84, 86

Sumer, astronomers of, 104

Surveying, 30, 98–99

Système International d'Unités (SI), 101, 102, 104, 105

Table of Weights and Measures, U.S., 98

Tallies, in vaults of British Parliament, 61

Technology, 71

Telegraph, and Atlantic cable, 71

Television, as means of conveying information on metric system, 109

Temperature, measurement of, 101–103

Thermometers, 102–103

Time, measurement of, 20, 103–105

Time zones, 81

Tolerances, close, in production of goods, 89

Ton, 30, 85, 98

Treasury Department, U.S., 74

Treaty of the Meter (1875), 70, 105
Troy weight, 30

United Nations Conference on Human Environment (1972), 11

Vermont, U.S. measurement standards located in, during Civil War, 65
Verne, Jules, 70
Vitamins, dispensed in milligrams, 95
Volt, 101
Vulgar fractions, 99, 114

War of 1812, 55
Washington, George, 45

Water pollution, 12
Watt, James, 35, 109
Watt, as unit of power, 97, 101, 110
Weight, and mass, 100–101
Weights and measures, in early U.S., 24, 26, 27, 29–30
Whitney, Eli, 56

Yard, 16, 61, 65, 96; inaccuracy of British standard for, 61–62; measured by girth, 16; metric equivalent of, 12, 13; as nose-to-fingertip measure, 15

Zero, absolute, 103

ABOUT THE AUTHOR

For S. Carl Hirsch, as for many Americans, travel abroad was his first direct contact with the metric system. "It was one thing to be familiar as a science writer with cubic centimeters and degrees Celsius," writes Mr. Hirsch, "but it was another kind of challenge to speedily translate miles per gallon into kilometers per liter while motoring in France."

After finishing *Meter Means Measure,* Mr. Hirsch became involved in metric teaching with the Chicago Board of Education. Its radio station, WBEZ, has produced the series of scripts Mr. Hirsch has written called "Peter and the Meter."

Mr. Hirsch is the author of many popular books on science for young people. His books, *The Globe for the Space Age* and *The Living Community: A Venture into Ecology* have twice won him the Thomas Alva Edison Foundation Award, given annually for the best science book for children. Mr. Hirsch lives with his wife in Evanston, Illinois.